THE DOGGY DUNG DISASTER

& Other True Stories

Regular Kids Doing Heroic Things Around the World

Garth Sundem

free spirit
PUBLiSHiNG®

Helping kids
help themselves™
since 1983

Library of Congress Cataloging-in-Publication Data
Sundem, Garth.
    The doggy dung disaster & other true stories : regular kids doing heroic things around the world / Garth Sundem.
        p. cm.
    Includes bibliographical references.
    ISBN-13: 978-1-57542-216-9
    ISBN-10: 1-57542-216-6
    1. Child volunteers — Case studies. 2. Social action — Case studies. 3. Helping behavior in children — Case studies. 4. Altruism in children — Case studies. 5. Role models — Case studies. I. Title. II. Title: Doggy dung disaster and other true stories.
HQ784.V64S86 2006
302'.14 — dc22

                                                                    2006025377

The profiles in this book include information from media reports, Web sites, books, and other secondary sources. Every effort has been made to verify the accuracy of the book's content. All facts and figures cited are the most current available; all Web site URLs are accurate and active; and all have been verified as of August 2006. The author and Free Spirit Publishing make no warranty or guarantee concerning material from secondary sources and we are not responsible for any changes in Web site URLs that occur after this book's publication. If you find an error or believe that a resource listed here is not as described, please contact Free Spirit Publishing.

Image of dog on page 133: "© Photographer: Brandi Head, Agency: Dreamstime.com"

Edited by Douglas J. Fehlen
Cover design by Marieka Heinlen
Interior design by Jayne Curtis

10 9 8 7 6 5 4 3 2 1
Printed in the United States of America

Free Spirit Publishing Inc.
217 Fifth Avenue North, Suite 200
Minneapolis, MN 55401-1299
(612) 338-2068
help4kids@freespirit.com
www.freespirit.com

Free Spirit Publishing is a member of the Green Press Initiative, and we're committed to printing our books on recycled paper containing a minimum of 30% post-consumer waste (PCW). For every ton of books printed on 30% PCW recycled paper, we save 5.1 trees, 2,100 gallons of water, 114 gallons of oil, 18 pounds of air pollution, 1,230 kilowatt hours of energy, and .9 cubic yards of landfill space. At Free Spirit it's our goal to nurture not only young people, but nature too!

green press INITIATIVE

ACKNOWLEDGMENTS

Thanks to my family for carting me around the world as a child and helping me understand that while cultures differ, heroes are universal. Thanks also to Ms. Pikiewicz's sixth-grade classes in Bozeman, Montana, for their enthusiasm and insightful comments—keep writing!

CONTENTS

KIDS STANDING UP FOR THEMSELVES

KIDS HELPING OTHERS 59

KIDS OVERCOMING CHALLENGES 87

KIDS USING TALENTS AND CREATIVITY

FOREWORD

It's still a little weird to think of myself as a hero. After losing my left arm to a tiger shark on Halloween morning of 2003, I just kept living my life the best way I knew how. Sure, I tried to be brave, and sure, it was hard to get back in the water, but what choice did I have—it wasn't like I was never gonna surf again!

And as I read this book, I see 30 other young heroes who did the same thing. They're not crazy comic book characters born on some alien superhero planet or anything. These are kids, just like you and just like me, who faced a challenge head-on and chose to do something amazing—something we can all look at and be proud of.

In this book, you'll find kids who went looking for their challenges and others whose challenges found them (mine was a tiger shark—yikes!). And you'll see that not all heroes are six-foot-four muscle men in capes and funny suits. Heroes come in all sizes and all colors, and they live in every corner of the globe. I guess it doesn't matter who you are or even what your test is—it's what you do that matters. Do you let your challenge stop you, or do you use your courage, your creativity, your mind, and your heart to rise above?

So, am I a hero? Are any of the young people in this book heroes? Well, that's for you to decide! But I think we are all heroes—me, the other kids you'll read about, and *even you*—only, you might not know it yet!

— Bethany Hamilton

KIDS SAVING THE ENVIRONMENT

The Doggy Dung Disaster
HARUKA MARUNO

Would you believe that a 12-year-old Japanese girl was named one of nine "Heroes for the Planet" by *Time* magazine for picking up dog poop? What's even weirder is that this girl, like most people, *hated* picking up poop.

"It was gross," Haruka Maruno told *Time* magazine in 2000. Every morning when Haruka walked her dog, Patrick, she grimaced when she had to scoop his poop with a plastic bag over her hand. It felt warm and mushy, like a handful of, well . . . dog poop. Yuck!

But it turned out that cleaning up after Patrick with a plastic bag was more than just gross—it was also harming the environment. Just like they keep your sandwich fresh for lunch, plastic bags also keep animal waste from decomposing—breaking down back into the earth. Instead of becoming fertilizer, the poop-bag combo just sat in the local landfill looking disgusting, smelling bad, and taking up space.

Japan has over 10 million dogs, which produce over 2 million pounds of waste daily. That's a massive mountain of poop every day. Just imagine what the mountain might look like after a *month!* And because Japan is a small island, there isn't a lot of extra space. As much as people would have liked to keep mountains and mountains of dog poop sitting around, there just wasn't enough room. . . . Japan had a real doggy dung disaster.

Haruka Maruno decided to do something about it.

"What else could I use to scoop poop?" she thought. A shovel might work, but you couldn't just throw the whole shovel away. People would have to wash it when they were done—not very convenient. Maybe a plastic cup, but it might get a little messy, and messy was the *last* thing she wanted. Finally Haruka found a way to cut and fold an empty paper milk carton into the ultimate poop scoop.

The best part—other than being much less gross—was that the paper scoop allowed air and microbes to get in. You could throw the scoop away, and after a while everything would be gone, decomposed back into the earth like ice cream melting in the sun. No more taking up space in a landfill.

Goodbye, mountains of poop!

Haruka entered her "paperscoop" in an invention contest, held in her city of Miyakonojo. Her poop scoop won first prize! But that was not enough for Haruka. She thought about it: if only a few people knew about the paperscoop, it wouldn't get used enough to make a big difference. Haruka needed more than just a paperscoop stand on the corner if she wanted to win the battle against gross, smelly dog poop. She knew this was where her dad, Isamu, might be able to help. He was a businessman and helped Haruka set up her own company, which they called "Haruka Family."

eco-business:
An eco-business is a company that sells products that are not harmful to the environment.

Imagine what life is like for most seventh graders you know. Now imagine a seventh grader running a major **eco-business**. It wasn't easy! At 12 years old, Haruka Maruno was not only an inventor, but a sharp business-woman as well.

Every day, Haruka came home from school, grabbed a snack, and then got to work. She and her father had to find

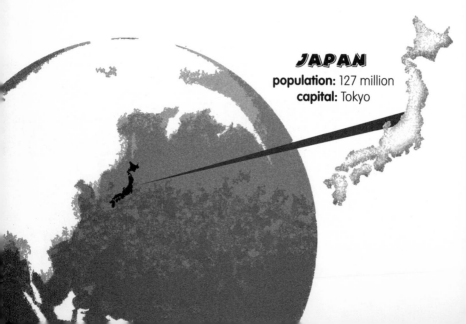

JAPAN
population: 127 million
capital: Tokyo

a factory that could turn recycled milk cartons into "Haruka's Paperscoops." They had to hire employees and keep detailed records of exactly what they sold and where. They also had to convince stores all over Japan to put a product on their shelves that encouraged people to get up close and personal with dog poop.

All of this hard work paid off. The poop scoop was a hit in stores. And the government of Japan took notice of the paperscoop and asked Haruka to represent Japan at the Children's Conference for the Environment in Africa. The conference, sponsored by the United Nations, gave Haruka the chance to talk about her special poop scoop with kids from many countries around the world.

Today, Haruka Maruno continues to run her business and work on inventions that help preserve the environment. You can be sure that the world will be a better place because of her work!

Haruka's Paperscoop is available at many pet supply stores in the United States and Canada. If you have a pooch, check for this special poop scoop at a store in your area.

The Longest Walk

OMAR CASTILLO GALLEGOS

Like citizens of many big cities, people in Mexico City do a lot of walking. Many walk to work or stroll to the bus stop. Others mosey to the grocery store or amble out at night to see movies and dine in restaurants. Kids jog down the block to visit friends and hike to city parks where they play soccer, baseball, and other games. However, the rainforest is 800 miles away from Mexico City, so people most certainly *do not* walk to the rainforest.

Unless, of course, you're eight-year-old Omar Castillo Gallegos.

One evening Omar watched a TV show about the destruction of the Mexican rainforest. He learned that up to 50,000 species a year become extinct as their rainforest habitat is slashed and burned to make room for farms. Omar also found out that only one-third of the world's rainforests remain, and that many people believe in 40 years there will be no rainforests left at all.

6

Though many people saw this same TV show, it was Omar who decided to do something about it.

But what could an eight-year-old boy do to stop a thousand bulldozers? He thought that if government leaders only knew about the destruction of the rainforests, they would have to do something to stop it. So Omar decided to write to the president of Mexico. Instead of putting the letter in the mail, he went to the president's palace and gave the letter to the guards standing outside.

The president agreed to save the rainforest and everybody lived happily ever after. . . .

Actually, that's not quite how it happened. After writing five letters and delivering each one to the guards outside the president's palace, Omar Castillo Gallegos still had received no response. He didn't even know if the president had *read* his letters.

"If it's that important to you," joked his father, "you should go to the rainforest and save it yourself."

Later that evening, Omar packed his bag. The next morning he was ready to leave for Chiapas, the Mexican state where the rainforest was being destroyed. Because he didn't want Omar to walk alone, Omar's father decided to go, too. He probably thought that Omar would get tired and want to return home before they got far. Once Omar started, though, he wasn't about to give up. The pair walked past Omar's neighborhood and through the streets of Mexico City. They reached the outskirts of the city, and then the suburbs, and still they kept walking. And walking. And walking. . . .

And then they walked some more. By the end of the first day they had walked almost 15 miles, and Omar's feet hurt. Only another 785 miles to go!

Day after day Omar and his father kept walking. Along the way something wonderful started to happen. One day, a woman came out to the road and offered Omar and his father food and water. She had heard about their journey to protect the rainforest, and she wanted to help. The next day, two people met Omar and his father on the road and offered them homemade tortillas. The day after that, a man offered them a place to sleep. Word of Omar and his father's walk was traveling faster than they were!

MEXICO
population: 107 million
capital: Mexico City

Now people came out to join Omar and his father on their walk. Instead of being just a hike, it was more like a parade. And as people came from all over to see this eight-year-old who was walking 800 miles, the parade grew!

Finally, after three pairs of shoes, 800 miles, and 39 days of walking, Omar, his father, and the parade came to the town in Chiapas where the governor lived. Omar led his followers to the steps of the governor's palace and yelled with all his might, "Save the rainforest!" He yelled again and again, "Save the rainforest!" Omar's father and all the people who had followed them to the governor's palace also yelled, "Save the rainforest!"

Finally, the governor came out onto the balcony of his palace and the crowd fell silent. The governor looked down at Omar Castillo Gallegos and his father and said, "I'm sorry, but if you want to save the rainforest, you will have to talk with the president of Mexico, who lives in Mexico City."

Omar and his father had just walked 800 miles *from* Mexico City, where they had already tried to make contact with the president. Now they were tired and sore and it looked like they would have to walk all the way home. But they had not counted on the support of others. People all over Mexico had heard about their mission, and someone bought Omar and his father bus tickets back to Mexico City.

Mexico City!?!

But once Omar Castillo Gallegos had made up his mind to save the rainforest, it would take more than this little setback to stop him. He pitched a tent outside the president's palace, and during the day he walked around shouting, "I want to meet with the president so that he will save the rainforest!"

Other kids joined him, and other adults, too. Soon TV news crews showed up to report on the small "city" that had sprung up on the brick square outside the palace. The president could ignore them no longer. He invited Omar to meet with him. After talking with eight-year-old Omar Castillo Gallegos, the president of Mexico decided to protect the Chiapas rainforest. All it took was an 800-mile walk!

But it turned out that helping protect the rainforest was only Omar's first step. Once he had the ear of the people in charge, he realized there were many other things in the world that needed saving. So, he organized more than 5,000 children in Cancun to stop the destruction of Lake Nichupte. Next, he talked the secretary of education into including the study of the environment in all of Mexico's textbooks. Then he biked to nine Mexican states, visiting lakes, rivers, and seas to teach people about water pollution.

Imagine the pairs of shoes that he must have worn through!

Turtle Power

HENRY CILLEY

Henry Cilley lived in a suburb of Chicago where new buildings sprang up every day. It seemed like he could ride past an open field on the way to school, and on the way home there would be five department stores, a couple of fast-food joints, a movie theater, and a gas station. Many people called this "progress."

But Henry Cilley was not "many people." In his opinion, progress and *pavement* didn't have to go together.

In 2001, Henry's third-grade teacher read the class a newspaper article about construction that was due to start in nearby Lake in the Hills. This construction would be next to the 117-acre Exner Marsh Nature Preserve. Unfortunately, many of the endangered Blanding's turtles that lived in the marsh would soon find their nesting sites paved over. Turtles could be squished by cars if they wandered onto the parking lot. Or poisoned by the gross sludge that would likely wash into the marsh.

Many students in Henry Cilley's class wanted to save the Blanding's turtles. They wrote letters to the Lake in the Hills village president asking him to stop the construction. One of the teaching assistants in Henry's class, who lived near the village president, personally delivered the letters. The class never got a response.

"That's when Henry started to bug the living daylights out of me about what was going to happen to the turtles," remembers Henry's mom, Katherine. But what could they do? Henry and his mom called the Illinois Nature Preserves Commission, a group set up to protect natural habitats from overdevelopment. "They said it was a done deal," recalls Henry's mom. "They said there was nothing we could do."

And that's when Henry Cilley kicked into high gear.

Henry decided to start a petition. He thought if he gathered enough signatures from people who wanted to save the turtles of Exner Marsh, the construction company and the Lake in the Hills community wouldn't be able to ignore them the way they had ignored the

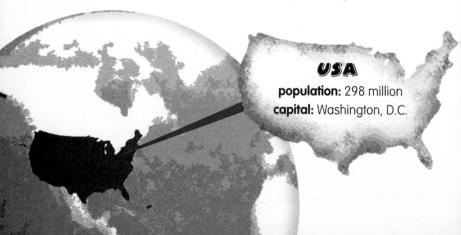

USA
population: 298 million
capital: Washington, D.C.

letters from his class. He started collecting signatures at school open houses where his classmates' parents signed the petition. Then he stood outside grocery stores with a clipboard and a pen, asking shoppers to take 30 seconds to help save the turtles.

Soon, the Cub Scouts in town heard about Exner Marsh, the construction, and Henry's petition. Interested in his cause, the scouts invited Henry to speak at a citywide scout gathering. There was only one problem—the thought of speaking in front of more than 250 people made Henry want to lock himself in a closet! He was a quiet, soft-spoken kid who would rather have faced 250 hungry grizzly bears than 250 Cub Scouts. What would he say? Everybody would be looking at him—what would happen if his voice cracked or if he tripped on his way to the stage? Would people laugh? Would they boo?

Then Henry had another thought—what would happen if he didn't speak? The turtles could die, that's what. And with this thought, Henry made up his mind—he would have to give the speech.

When the big day came, Henry was nervous. In front of the scouting group, he felt like he stuttered and stopped and started and said *ummmm* too many times. He worried he'd totally blown it. At the end of the speech, he waited for people to start booing or throwing rotten tomatoes. Instead, they clapped. Not only did they clap, they gave him a standing ovation.

Bravo, Henry!

The Cub Scouts were so impressed with Henry that they decided to help him gather signatures for his petition to save Exner Marsh. When all was said and done, Henry and the scouts had gathered more than 700 signatures on what came to be called the "Friends of Henry" petition. But when Henry gave his petition to the president of the Lake in the Hills village board, he refused to read it! Because most of the people who had signed the Friends of Henry petition lived outside the Lake in the Hills neighborhood, their signatures were useless.

It looked like all the work that Henry and the scouts had put into gathering signatures would be for nothing. And it looked like the turtles were doomed.

But Henry still wouldn't give up. He and his mother again contacted the Illinois Nature Preserves Commission (the same people who had said the construction was a "done deal") and told them about the Friends of Henry petition, the 700 signatures, and the Lake in the Hills village board. By this time Henry Cilley's story had also been published in the local paper. More and more people were learning about the Blanding's turtles and Exner Marsh, and public pressure to stop the development was growing.

After Henry's second call, the Preserves Commission contacted the construction company to talk turtles. After negotiations, the construction company agreed to work with Henry and the other preservation groups to make sure the development would be turtle-friendly.

Following the advice of Preserves Commission experts, the construction company built six turtle nesting sites on their property around the marsh, and installed a high curb to make sure the turtles couldn't wander onto the parking lot. The company also built fencing to make sure trash from the parking lot didn't blow into the marsh. It installed a series of filters to make sure water that washed off the parking lot would be clean by the time it reached the marsh. And fines starting at $2,500 for disturbing turtle eggs were set to keep people away from the nests. The construction company also agreed to not build on 10 acres of land so there would be some space between the development and Exner Marsh.

The turtles were saved! It turned out the construction company didn't have anything against turtles — it just needed to be reminded by someone how important Exner Marsh was. That someone was Henry Cilley.

As for Henry, today he is a seventh grader, an A student, and a frog monitor at his local wetlands. Henry knows that while he succeeded in saving the Blanding's turtles in his town, there are thousands of places across the country just like Exner Marsh where development threatens natural habitats. If you look closely, you might be able to find an Exner Marsh in your own community. And when you do, remember Henry Cilley and get involved!

Here's a tip: Visit www.idealist.org to find suggestions for making a difference in your neighborhood.

Plastic
Bags Sacked

HARSHIT AGRAWAL

Have you ever seen jellyfish? They are big clear blobs that float through the ocean like drifting parachutes, entangling prey in their long tentacles. If you were a sea turtle, jellyfish would look like lunch.

Have you ever seen plastic bags? They are big clear blobs that float through the ocean like drifting para-chutes, entangling prey in their long handles. If you were a sea turtle, plastic bags would look like lunch, too.

Plastic bags are dangerous!

Unfortunately, if you were a sea turtle and you ate a plastic bag instead of a jellyfish, you would be toast. More than 100,000 sea animals die every year from eating or get-ting tangled in plastics. According to www.turtles.org, one out of every three dead turtles that washed ashore between 1979 and 1988 had plastic in its stomach.

And since then plastic-bag use has only increased. Today, 4 *trillion* to 5 *trillion* plastic bags are made *every year*. That's an average of about 570 bags for each person on Earth, every year. And like diamonds, a plastic bag is forever. Paper, cloth, and cardboard biodegrade, or break down back into the earth. Plastic doesn't. Bags made of plastic just sit around in landfills or float through the water looking like a sea turtle's lunch. One thousand years from now, the same plastic bag will still be floating around the ocean — that is, if it's not eaten first.

And it's not just sea life that is endangered by plastic litter. In Bangladesh, plastic bags clogged storm grates and caused flooding. In New Delhi, India, 18 deer died in Bannerghatta Park after eating plastic bags.

For 10-year-old Harshit Agrawal, from New Delhi, the deaths of the deer were the last straw. He decided to do something about the out-of-control plastic-bag use in his city. But Harshit knew that simply switching to paper bags wasn't the answer. While plastic bags are bad for the environment, paper bags aren't much better. It takes trees and energy to make a paper bag. Also, a paper bag costs about four cents to make, while a plastic bag costs only one cent. Harshit Agrawal thought the answer was to bring a reusable cloth bag to the grocery store. This way there would be no waste.

Harshit started a club, the Little Eco Friends, dedicated to helping preserve the environment. It was a group of 9- to 13-year-olds from his neighborhood of Sheshadhripuram. Together they made cloth bags out of old clothes and gave them to whoever would take them. People loved the new cloth bags, but it took about two hours to make a bag. At that rate it would take the eight Little Eco Friends about 28,000 years to make a bag for each person in India—way too long! They needed a way to get more people to use cloth bags of their own.

Where do people get plastic bags, thought Harshit. He pictured Nilgris, the department store in his neighborhood. People there bought clothes, clocks, and purses—all carried home in plastic. Every day hundreds of people went in and out of the store, and every day they used thousands of plastic bags. Harshit went to Nilgris to see what could be done. He talked to the checkout clerk, who sent him to the manager, who finally sent him to the storeowner.

Harshit told the owner about plastic bags, about the turtles in the ocean, and about the deer in the park. The owner of the store agreed to help by offering a one-percent discount to shoppers who packed their

INDIA
population: 1.1 billion
capital: New Delhi

purchases in cloth bags. It was a small victory, but an important one. Soon, shoppers started bringing their own bags to Nilgris. They felt good about saving money and great about helping protect the environment.

Next, Harshit thought, *where do people carry plastic bags? Well,* he thought, *in the street on their way to and from stores, of course!* So the Little Eco Friends took to the streets, too. To spread their message, they performed street plays and organized marches. Each member of the Little Eco Friends told people they knew about the dangers of plastic bags. Once people learned how bad plastic bags were for the environment, they began to use fewer of them. Safdar Andoor's father stopped carrying office files in plastic bags. Ankush Bagrecha's pharmacist stopped giving out medications in plastic bags. And Karan Singhvi's mother carried only cloth bags when shopping for groceries.

Harshit saw his club grow from a group of eight to a group of more than 500 volunteers. Today, the Little Eco Friends not only educate others about plastic use, they also plant trees and organize cleanups of parks and schools. They teach people how to conserve water and reuse items that usually end up in landfills.

In 2002, the Little Eco Friends won the Volvo Environment Prize. Harshit and the eight original members flew to Sweden to collect the $10,000 award. Do you think the Little Eco Friends blew the winnings on new bikes, MP3 players, and video games? Actually, they donated all their winnings to a new campaign to clean up the polluted lakes of New Delhi.

Show Me the Water!

AMY BEAL

If you wanted to know about the brush-tailed bettong, long-nosed poteroo, or southern hairy-nosed wombat, Amy Beal would be the person to ask. These animals are marsupials—and Amy happens to be an expert. She has been building houses and digging tunnels for these endangered Australian animals since she was 12 years old.

Amy came to know all things marsupial by joining a club at her school. She learned from older friends how to bottle-feed a motherless ring-tailed possum, how to weigh and microchip a greater bilby, and how to make a wool pouch where young orphaned marsupials can safely grow. When taking care of a newborn, Amy even wore her wool pouch to class! When she became one of the older students in the club, Amy loved to pass on her knowledge to new members.

But helping marsupials and teaching others about them weren't the only things that Amy Beal did to help protect the Australian environment. She recycled her family's trash and helped her grandmother replant her farm with native species that could grow in the dry Australian climate. Amy also spoke to groups visiting the Adelaide Zoo and took animals around to local classrooms. It was important to her that others knew about the **ecosystems** of the region and how they could help protect them.

But what really got Amy Beal thinking was water. And it wasn't because she was thirsty. "Adelaide is the driest state in the driest country in the world," she said. The whole *region* was thirsty!

ecosystems: Ecosystems are environments where plants and animals live together in balance.

Most of the water in Adelaide comes from one place—the Murray River. And because the Murray River is the only fresh water around, it is used for everything. Farmers use it to water their fields. The government uses it to generate electricity. People drink from reservoirs filled by the river. And when it is hot—which is almost always—people waterski, swim, and fish in its cool waters.

Amy attended the International River Health Conference, where she and kids from around the world learned more about the Murray River. They discovered the biggest problem was that once people took water out for all those things, there wasn't enough left for the river! That is why thousands of red gum trees were dying along its banks. And why fish were being left high and dry, unable to spawn in the shallows.

Even though the problem was obvious, nobody could agree on what to do. Some people wanted the farmers to use less water. The farmers thought people should take shorter showers. And the government told people in the region that if they wanted electricity, they would have to deal with the effects of dams on the Murray.

The only people Amy Beal could find who still had an open mind were the kids at her school, and what could *they* do to save the Murray River? Amy wasn't sure. But she did know that one day her generation would lead the country and she thought she could help make sure these young leaders had the welfare of the Murray River in mind when that day came.

AUSTRALIA
population: 20 million
capital: Canberra

Amy could have started by teaching one or two kids at a time, but she wanted to do more. She wished all the kids in her area could have been at the International River Health Conference, and she wondered if it might be possible to organize a similar conference in her city of Adelaide. Amy decided to find out.

She told her school and all the schools in the area that she was holding a kids' conference about the Murray River. Amy hung flyers and called parents and made sure that every school talked about her conference during the morning announcements. She scheduled a meeting room and created sign-up forms. And because she didn't want her conference to be just another day at school, she decided there wouldn't be any teachers.

The whole conference would be kids teaching kids, just like in the marsupial club, so Amy gathered student volunteers to teach classes. And she made sure that each volunteer designed a fun lesson that would get people excited about preserving the river.

When the conference opened, more than 200 kids showed up to learn about the Murray River! Amy took them to see the dry, cracked mud at the edge of the river where whole forests of red gum trees had turned gray. The kids waded all the way across the river without getting their shorts wet because the water was so shallow. Another student taught five ways to conserve water. Another taught kids how to recognize the footprints of endangered species along the muddy riverbanks.

Amy's conference was a huge success. And, in 2003, thanks to people like Amy Beal speaking up about poor river health, the Australian government announced an improvement program for the Murray River. The 15 goals of this program included protection of animals and plants that depend on the river and a reduction in the use of pesticides and other pollutants.

Amy's conference went so well she turned it into a club where kids could keep learning about water quality and conservation. For her efforts, Amy was a finalist for the 2004 Australian Young Person of the Year Award. About her future, Amy says, "Nothing's too hard. What's next? Who knows—wherever my heart takes me I suppose!"

Comic
Book Hero
AIKA TSUBOTA

Have you ever wanted to make your own comic book? Aika Tsubota did.

From the time she was five years old, Aika wrote stories, created characters, and made them into comic strips. She shared these creations with her family and friends. Aika drew comics about animals and things that happened to her at school. She also made up comics about things she could only imagine—like unicorns and space aliens. She was a gifted artist, and her family thought that someday her comic books might be in every supermarket and toy store in Japan.

Aika was also concerned about the environment. When she was 10, she wrote, *I think of the earth as a gentle cradle that watches over all of the lives on it.*

The next year, when Aika was in the sixth grade, her teacher assigned a special project. Students could do whatever they wanted as long as they finished before winter break.

For her project, Aika Tsubota drew a comic book.

And she poured her heart into this book like no other project. Aika drew late at night until her mother insisted she go to sleep. She checked out dozens of books from the library to learn more about the environment. She sculpted each page until it was perfect. Aika made sure her comic book was funny, informative, and easy to understand. When her friends asked her to play or to go to the movies, Aika said she would love to—as soon as she finished her comic book.

Did she know this book would be her last?

When you read Aika's *Secrets of the Earth*, you meet a boy named Eiichi and a girl named Rumi. Rumi checks out a library book, and when the two kids open it, out jumps the earth. "Hi, there!" says Earth, before taking Eiichi and Rumi on a magical tour of the environment.

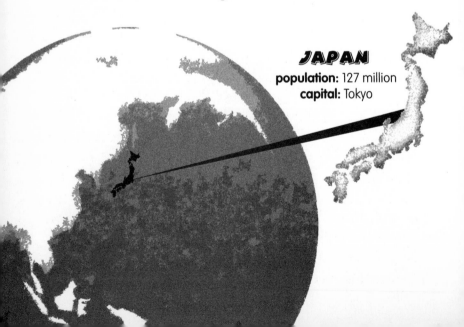

JAPAN
population: 127 million
capital: Tokyo

They visit the weather, the soil, and the oceans. They talk about things that threaten Earth — like acid rain, pollution, and a fragile **ozone layer**.

We need to keep working until not even one person harms the earth, wrote Aika at the end of her book. *If everyone in the world did a small part, the earth would be saved overnight. I wish that every person could see that we need to save this beautiful planet.*

Finally Aika was finished with *Secrets of the Earth* and she handed it in to her teacher. It was a masterpiece.

Aika died about one week after she finished *Secrets of the Earth*. A blood vessel in her brain had burst. She was only 12 years old.

ozone layer:
The ozone layer is a blanket of gas around the earth that protects us from the sun's heat.

This, of course, is where Aika's story ends, but it is not the end of *Secrets of the Earth*. Aika's parents made 50 copies of her comic book and gave them to her friends and teachers to help them remember their friend Aika. These people made copies and gave them to *their* friends. Aika's comic book spread slowly from person to person, gaining momentum like a rolling snowball.

Eventually, Japanese newspapers wrote about Aika's story and her little comic book. The press coverage allowed others to learn about *Secrets of the Earth* — including the Foundation for Global Peace and Environment. The organization started publishing Aika's book and soon it seemed like everyone in Japan had a copy. Schools began using *Secrets of the Earth* as a textbook in science classes. The comic was so good that it wasn't long before it was translated into Chinese, English, Arabic, French, Korean, Vietnamese, Thai, and German.

Aika's parents had believed that one day their daughter's comic books would be sold in supermarkets and toy stores all over Japan. They never guessed, though, that Aika's work would be a hit all over the world! In fact, there are now more than 500,000 copies of *Secrets of the Earth* in print. The book has been made into an animated cartoon and a musical. At an Earth Summit, the governor of Aika's province in Japan distributed copies of the comic book to the leaders of the world.

In the few days between the completion of her book and the end of her life, Aika wrote: *The most important thing is for people to stop feeling powerless because they are only one person. You can make a difference! If everybody pitches in, I know we can turn this planet into a beautiful place.*

KIDS STANDING UP FOR THEMSELVES

Top of the World
SANTOSH YADAV

Girls can't climb mountains.

At least that's what people told Santosh Yadav while she was growing up in the small village of Haryana in India.

"Girls can't climb mountains," said her parents.

"Girls can't climb mountains," said her five older brothers.

"Girls can't climb mountains," said her cousins and aunts and uncles and grandparents.

Even her neighbors and schoolteachers said that *girls can't climb mountains.*

And until she was 14 years old, Santosh believed them. She had never even seen snow, let alone thought about climbing through it to the top of a mountain. Most girls who lived in her village didn't go to school past the second grade, so they didn't even know there *were* mountains. For these girls, just going to the market was a rare treat.

But one thing made Santosh different from the other girls in her village—she fought to stay in school. Her brothers went to a good school in a nearby town, but it was not open to girls. Instead, Santosh had to walk almost three miles to the small village school. When it rained during her walk, she made a hat out of her book bag. While in class, she sat on the bag because there was not anything else to sit on. She was the only girl.

In school, Santosh read books and looked at magazines and saw pictures of towering mountains topped with snow. She learned there were mountains not far from where she lived. In fact, the Himalayas, home to the tallest mountains in the world, were just on the border between India and Nepal. She read a magazine article about climbers who tested themselves against the world's tallest mountain—Mt. Everest.

Santosh talked her family into visiting the mountains during one school break. She wanted to see with her own eyes what she had read about in magazines.

When her family got to the mountains, Santosh's five older brothers talked about India's famous climbers. Some had reached the top of Mt. Everest. Her brothers thought maybe they would become famous mountain climbers, too. As her brothers spouted names, Santosh noticed that all the climbers they talked about were men.

"Someday *I'd* like to climb Mt. Everest," said Santosh.

"Well, that's cute," said her father, "but everybody knows that girls can't climb mountains." Besides, everybody in the village knew that Santosh would be getting married soon. After all, she was 16, and that's when a girl's father was supposed to choose her husband. According to everybody, Santosh wouldn't have time to climb mountains because she would be starting a family. Santosh didn't say anything else that day, but inside she decided to prove *everybody* wrong.

And she started training to be a mountain climber.

Every day after school, she went for a run and whenever she could, she visited the small, nearby Aravali Hills. Sometimes the local climbers would teach her knots for climbing ropes and how to use the ropes to catch a falling climber. Little by little, Santosh got stronger and stronger. When she wasn't training, she was drawing pictures of mountains.

The people in her village thought she was crazy because they knew that *girls can't climb mountains*. They wondered what she was doing running around in

INDIA
population: 1.1 billion
capital: New Delhi

shorts, huffing and puffing, when she should be getting ready to have a family.

Whenever Santosh got money, even a small amount, she would stash it away. Now she used it to enroll in a mountain climbing class. *Paying good money for a useless dream?* said the people of the village. They couldn't believe it!

Finally her father had had enough. He decided to put an end to Santosh's mountain-climbing dreams. But before you label him this story's bad guy, imagine what it must have been like for him! Every person in the village looked sideways at him and whispered about Santosh behind his back. Not only did they whisper about Santosh, but they also said *what a bad father — what a disgraceful family! How could he have raised such a willful girl?* He loved his daughter and wanted her to be happy, but what was he to do?

He decided that he would go to the first day of Santosh's mountain-climbing class and drag her home. As soon as they got home, he would lock Santosh in her room until he could find her a husband — preferably someone who had never heard of mountain climbing. But as Santosh's father stormed out of the house on the way to the class, he slipped, fell down the stairs, and broke his ankle.

You would think that the father of a mountain climber would be a little more coordinated!

After his fall, Santosh's father gave up trying to pressure her. Santosh stayed in the mountain-climbing class. She didn't get married, and her family members and neighbors remained upset. They thought if a young woman was still unmarried by the time she was 17, she would certainly grow old sad and lonely without any family at all. Santosh had passed up getting married and everything *normal* for an impossible dream. After all, everyone knew that girls couldn't climb mountains.

What must everyone from the village have thought when Santosh became the first Indian woman to climb Mt. Everest? Here's what Santosh thought: "It was magical," she said. "I still get goose pimples thinking of the moment. The feeling is indescribable. The Indian flag was flying on top of the world. I felt proud as an Indian." And Santosh Yadav climbed Mt. Everest again to become the first woman ever to stand on the top of the world *twice*.

You might think that Santosh would credit her success to strong legs or lungs of steel, but she says, "Education is the key." If she hadn't fought to stay in school, she says, she never would have known that mountains existed. And she never would have started dreaming about climbing them.

With Santosh as a role model, more young girls are sure to stay in school and learn to dream, too. They may even look up at Mt. Everest, and when they ask about it, their parents and older brothers and neighbors and uncles will say, "Yes, dear, girls *can* climb mountains."

When Small Voices Unite

FARLIZ CALLE AND THE COLOMBIAN CHILDREN FOR PEACE

In 1996, Farliz Calle was 15 years old. She had a wide smile and sparkling eyes and was the president of her student council. Farliz's father picked bananas at a nearby plantation and her mother cooked for the plantation workers. She had two sisters, a brother, and many friends. Farliz wanted to go to college and become a criminal psychologist when she grew up. It was impossible not to like Farliz Calle.

But like most teenagers, Farliz had problems, too. If you have ever been to middle school or had a pimple or been born, then you can probably relate to the problems that most young people have. However, Farliz's difficulties were a little different—she worried about her father. "I dream that one day I will wake up and my father will go to work and I will not have the fear that he will be shot," Farliz said.

And it was not just her father she worried about. All of the people of Apartadó, Colombia—adults and children—were in danger. There had been fighting in the country for over 50 years. During that time, more than 300,000 people had died. Much of the death and destruction had been caused by fighting between the government and drug gangs. In the capital city of Bogotá, car bombs and kidnappings were common.

Despite living her entire life with violence around her, Farliz kept hope in her heart that someday the children of Colombia would sleep through nights without being awoken by gunfire. She could imagine a time when kids could play outside without fear of being kidnapped by gangs. But what more could she do?

COLOMBIA
population: 44 million
capital: Bogotá

As president of the student council at her school, Farliz could organize assemblies. She could try to get better food in the cafeteria or new sports equipment for recess. But she couldn't stop the fighting, could she? Farliz decided to find out.

When a United Nations representative named Graca Machel visited Apartadó to gather information about how war affects children, Farliz helped organize a greeting for her that included an exhibition of poems, letters, paintings, sculptures, and stories—all by children. The creations showed the effects of war on kids as well as kids' hopes for peace. In all, more than 5,000 children participated in this Week of Reflection. Farliz Calle read Ms. Machel a letter written by the children of Apartadó. It asked the adults "for peace in our homes, for them not to make orphans of children, to allow us to play freely in the streets, and for no harm to come to our small brothers and sisters."

Graca Machel was moved by the children's work. When she reported back to the United Nations, the struggle of Colombia's children burst onto the world stage.

The Children's Peace Movement was born.

And as soon as the movement began, Farliz found others who wanted to help. Like Juan Elias Uribe, who wanted peace on behalf of his father, a doctor who was killed when he spoke out against the violence. And Mayerly Sanchez, who stepped up to help after her best friend was murdered by a Colombian gang. Wolfrido Zambrano signed on to help because he was tired of seeing dead bodies in the streets of Apartadó. Dilio Lorenzo, another participant, said, "Enough is enough and we won't accept this anymore. We demand change." None of these members were over 16 years old.

The first thing Farliz and the other leaders of the Children's Peace Movement noticed is that they had quickly outgrown student government. Under the Colombian constitution, citizens could elect a mayor and form their own local government. That's just what the young leaders of the group did. With Farliz as mayor, they began organizing carnivals for children who had been forced from their homes by violence.

As the Children's Peace Movement got bigger, Farliz noticed that people always seemed to be voting for something—a new judge, new taxes, new laws, more money for the army. But none of these things seemed as important to Farliz and her friends as peace.

Why not vote for peace? thought Farliz.

Peace? I like the sound of that!

The group set a goal. In only six months, they wanted to get 500,000 kids around the country to vote for their right to peace. Farliz thought that if enough children spoke out, their government and the governments of the world would have to listen.

After a lot of hard work getting the word out about the vote and connecting with other kids around the country, the group met its goal—and then some! On October 25, 1996, after only six months of organization, the Children's Peace Movement got 2.7 million young people to vote for the right to "survival, peace, family, and freedom from abuse."

But not everybody was happy with the Children's Peace Movement, and this included some of the country's most dangerous people. Farliz said, "I never speak out against any particular group. If I did, then I know I could become a target. All the children in the peace movement know that they must be careful about what they say." Even so, the leaders received daily death threats.

Despite the danger, Farliz and the other young leaders continued to work for peace—and this included working with the adults in the country. One year after the historic children's vote, Colombia's adults held their own vote. Ten million adults from the country voted for peace. Today violence in Colombia is decreasing, but much work still needs to be done.

After being nominated for the Nobel Peace Prize in 1999, Farliz was invited to speak at events all over the world. At a peace conference in the Netherlands, Farliz summed up the goals of the Children's Peace Movement:

"We request to all the adults of all the countries in the world:

Peace in the world.

Peace in our countries.

Peace in our homes.

Peace in our hearts."

Come Together
IVAN SEKULOVIC & PETRIT SELIMI

What if your parents made you stop hanging out with anyone who had blonde hair? Or green eyes? Or any person who was a little different from you in some way? What if some kids weren't allowed in school? Or their families were forced to leave the country?

Something like this happened in Serbia, but it wasn't hair or eye color that was the issue. Instead, people of two different ethnic groups, the Serbians and the Albanians, didn't get along. The Serbians were in charge and treated Albanians unfairly. The Albanians weren't allowed to go to school, they were fired from jobs, and they couldn't participate in the government.

One place where this tension was very strong was in the city of Prishtina, where Petrit Selimi and Ivan Sekulovic lived. Petrit was Albanian and Ivan was a Serb. According to all the adults in the country, the two 15-year-olds should have hated each other. But Petrit and Ivan saw no reason to hate. They were good friends and enjoyed playing soccer together or just hanging out. It didn't matter that one was Albanian and one Serbian.

So it was hard for the two friends in 1996 when fighting broke out. The Albanians believed they were standing up for their rights. The Serbian government called them terrorists. It was a complicated situation. If you had walked down the Prishtina streets during this time, you would have seen bullet holes in the concrete walls. You would have watched the windows above you in case someone decided to poke out a gun and try to put a hole in you, too.

Ivan and Petrit didn't care if the Serbs or the Albanians were right or wrong, they just wanted the violence to stop. So the two boys started a group for kids who were fed up with the fighting. Once a week the group met in an old, run-down house to talk peace. These meetings were not always safe. There were adults on both sides who wanted them stopped. Those adults couldn't believe their children were meeting with kids from the other group. They forbade their children to attend meetings.

Instead of falling apart amidst the danger and tension, Ivan, Petrit, and the group only grew stronger.

Soon the group started to do more than just talk peace. They organized art classes and plays—even a graffiti workshop—that taught kids to spread the message of peace. They wanted to replace the messages of war that were sprayed in red on the cement walls of the cities. Together Ivan Sekulovic and Petrit Selimi did everything they could do to bring together Albanians and Serbs.

It wasn't enough. In 1999, civil war came to Prishtina.

Fighting between Albanians and Serbs broke out in the streets and international warplanes flew over the city. Still, Ivan and Petrit refused to quit. Instead, they planned their most ambitious project yet. The two called out to young people, both Albanian and Serbian, to help clean up and repair the Boro and Ramiz Sports Center. The sports center was a place named after one Serb and one Albanian hero from World War II. It was a place where both groups of kids shared memories of soccer practice and other sports in the peaceful past. If they could work together to repair the sports center, maybe they could work together to repair the country, too.

SERBIA
population: 9 million
capital: Belgrade

On a day when gunshots echoed through the city and people threw rocks at tanks, 600 Albanian and Serbian kids showed up at the Boro and Ramiz Sports Center. They were ready to work. For a week, they cleaned and scrubbed. They pulled out old carpet, repainted cracked walls, and cleared debris off long-forgotten basketball courts. Each morning 600 kids showed up and worked like they had never worked before — like their country depended on it. And with each wheelbarrow load of broken cement, Petrit Selimi, Ivan Sekulovic, and their friends uncovered a little of their country's past.

At the end of the week, the Boro and Ramiz Sports Center was almost perfect. It looked like the old days, before the war, before Serbs and Albanians fought and destroyed everything that was good in the country. When the dust settled, the group opened their arms and showed the city of Prishtina what Serbs and Albanians could do if they worked together.

For six months, kids from both groups played soccer and basketball and other games peacefully with one another at the sports complex. Unfortunately, the war continued to cause destruction and, on the night of February 2, 2000, the sports complex burned to the ground. Do you think Petrit and Ivan wasted their time?

Today there is still tension between the Albanians and the Serbs of Prishtina, but there are 600 people, now young adults, who have experienced the power of peace with their own hands. And that is something that no amount of fire can burn away.

U.S.A.

Get Up, Stand Up

MALIKA SANDERS

Malika Sanders grew up with racism.

And in her hometown of Selma, Alabama, discrimination didn't stop at name-calling. When Malika was 15, she noticed something strange in her school—some classes included all white students and others all black students. Malika checked it out and learned that the classes with white kids were mostly advanced. The classes with black kids were remedial. Malika was a good student, and so it seemed strange to her that she had been placed in less-advanced classes.

After further investigation, she found out more. Teachers, who were supposedly grouping students based on ability, were actually grouping students based on race. All the black students were going into one set of classes and the white kids were going into another. This was segregation of the schools—something that had been made illegal in 1954.

How could this be happening?

Malika took action by starting a group called SMART—Student Movement Against Racial Tracking. ("Tracking" is a way to group students in classrooms.) She taught students and parents about racial tracking, and she led demonstrations demanding quality education for all. After a year, nothing had changed. Malika and her African-American friends were still being placed in low-level classes—even if they were really good at a subject and belonged in an advanced class. Something drastic had to be done.

Malika organized a peaceful sit-in where students parked themselves in the hallways and refused to move. They caused the school to close for five days. Finally, the city could no longer ignore the issue of racial tracking. In 1996 the city of Selma, Alabama, began testing students for class placement, ensuring that students of all races would have an equal chance of being chosen for advanced classes.

Forefront, an organization dedicated to defending human rights, reported that "it was an important victory for the children of Selma," but Malika knew it was only the beginning.

Growing up, Malika Sanders had thought long and hard about racial equality. "I can remember being aware of injustice and inequality even as a little girl and wanting to find solutions," she remembers. Civil rights became a passion for her. "By the time I was 12, I knew it was going to be my life's work."

It didn't hurt that her parents were both important community leaders. They began fighting for civil rights in the 1960s. Since that time, some things in Selma had gotten better. Others hadn't changed at all. For example, Joe Smitherman, who had called Dr. Martin Luther King Jr. a racist name on national television, was still mayor. And when Rose Sanders was about to vote against Joe Smitherman in the 2000 election, she was met by six police officers who tried to stop her.

This might have had something to do with her daughter, Malika. . . .

By this time Malika Sanders had joined the 21st Century Youth Leadership Movement and had organized the "Joe's Gotta Go" campaign. As Malika said, "Democracy was nowhere to be found in Joe Smitherman's Selma. Things had to change." She knew that many people in Selma, both black and white, wanted Joe

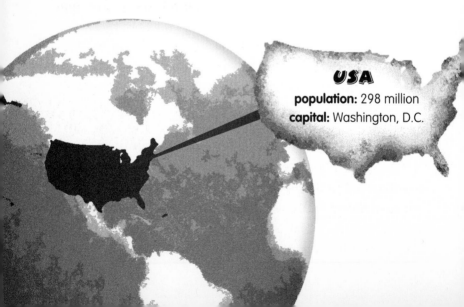

USA
population: 298 million
capital: Washington, D.C.

Smitherman gone. But it seemed like the only people who actually showed up to vote at every election were Smitherman supporters. Malika thought that if she could only convince *everyone* in Selma to vote, then Mayor Joe would have to go.

Malika started the Joe's Gotta Go campaign by standing on a street corner holding a sign. At first, maybe only one or two cars in an afternoon honked their horns in support. Malika remembered, "They certainly weren't ready to go up against the notorious Joe T. Smitherman."

Then things started to change. "It started as a trickle," Malika said, with only a few cars in an afternoon honking in support of the Joe's Gotta Go signs. But then the trickle became a stream and the stream became a river. Soon people weren't just honking, they were stopping, getting out of their cars, and grabbing signs themselves.

Mayor Joe Smitherman responded with ads that said no white businesses would stay in Selma if there were a black mayor. Malika recalled, "Someone fire-bombed two cars at my parents' office. The cars had Joe's Gotta Go stickers on them. People understood they were being targeted."

The funny thing about all this is that Malika couldn't even vote—she wasn't 18. But she did know the votes of young people could make the difference in the election. Malika Sanders helped involve the hip-hop stars Queen Latifah, MC Lyte, and the Outlaws, who all recorded civil rights messages for the people of Selma. Malika and the 21st Century Youth Leadership Movement brought balloons and candy to high school football games and teen hangouts, telling young voters to "Get Your Vote On."

On election day, all kinds of people from every part of town came out to vote. It turned out that 80 percent of the people in Selma voted. And because of Malika's Joe's Gotta Go campaign, Joe Smitherman *went*.

Malika Sanders had won her battle, but she wants people to know that Selma isn't the only place where democracy needs help—there are many more places in the United States and around the world where inequality lives.

And in these places, it takes someone like Malika Sanders—or someone like *you*—to make things right. Will you stand up to defend fairness?

Living Proof
JEAN-DOMINIC LEVERSQUE-RENE

Ile Bizard (Bizard Island) in Quebec, Canada, is where the city of Montreal goes to play golf. Every weekend the small island's population of about 22,000 swells with mainlanders who drive across the bridge or take the small ferry from Ile Jesus. On Ile Bizard, golf courses take up about half the total area.

Jean-Dominic Leversque-Rene had lived among Ile Bizard's golf courses for all of his 10 years. One day, he recalled, "I was watching the *Simpsons* on television when I felt a lump on the right side of my neck."

At the hospital, doctors discovered that the lump was a tumor. Jean-Dominic had non-Hodgkin's lymphoma, a type of cancer. "Before, I had been thinking about going home and playing with my dog and my friends. Now, I was thinking about dying. I didn't want to die." The odds of surviving his kind of cancer were 50 percent.

While he was in the hospital, Jean-Dominic felt very alone. "I missed going to school and playing with my friends," he said. "I had a lot of time to think things over and to ask myself some questions." One of the questions he asked again and again was, *How could this happen to me?*

He found his answer while reading a flyer about his type of cancer. It could be caused by a common **pesticide** that is used to keep lawns green—the same one used by the many golf courses of Ile Bizard! Jean-Dominic started his fight to ban chemical pesticides the same week he started chemotherapy to fight his cancer.

But not everyone was as concerned as Jean-Dominic. The city officials of Ile Bizard refused to do

pesticides:
Pesticides are often used on lawns to kill unwanted bugs and plants. While pesticides can make lawns look nicer, those made from chemicals can be poisonous.

CANADA
population: 33 million
capital: Ottawa

anything about the chemicals used on golf courses. Jean-Dominic started protesting at city hall. "The time had come to do battle," he said. Every month he walked around the outside of the government building holding a sign that demanded the city council ban the use of pesticides. Soon the local newspapers wrote stories about Jean-Dominic, and other children joined his protests.

While he was protesting, Jean-Dominic Leversque-Rene was also fighting for his life. His chemotherapy used drugs to kill cancer cells. It's impossible to kill cancer cells without also killing some of the healthy cells around them. So the treatment for Jean-Dominic's non-Hodgkin's lymphoma made his hair fall out and made him feel sick all the time. He lost 30 pounds. "I was bald and looked like an old man," said Jean-Dominic. "I wore a baseball cap to cover my head."

Sick with infection after a round of chemotherapy, he overheard doctors tell his parents that he was not going to survive. Can you imagine how scared he must have been? And Jean-Dominic had already seen cancer take the lives of many of the friends he had made in the hospital. But if he died, who would continue the fight against pesticides?

"I understood then that my life was to have a greater purpose," he said. His struggle was not just for himself; it was for all the children with cancer caused by pesticides. This cause, he said, "helped me find the courage I needed to never give up the fight."

Jean-Dominic's campaign against pesticides was not successful overnight. During the fight for his life, he could still be found protesting outside city hall. When Jean-Dominic was too sick to walk, he sat with his sign. But he never gave up.

And though his protest had started small, Jean-Dominic soon found new ways to fight the use of dangerous chemicals. He gathered 15,000 signatures on a petition and toured Canada speaking to people in the government about the threats of pesticides. He even spoke to leaders from Canada, the United States, and Mexico who were making rules for the three countries as part of the North American Free Trade Agreement. Though you might never have met Jean-Dominic, he was fighting for you, too.

In 1997, the city council of Ile Bizard voted to ban the use of cosmetic pesticides, whose only purpose is to keep lawns green. In 2001, the city council went a step further. Due to the voice of Jean-Dominic and the people he moved to action, Ile Bizard banned the use of all pesticides on private lawns. The city also forced golf courses to reduce their pesticide use by 60 percent that year, with more reductions over the next four years. Influenced by Jean-Dominic's actions, other towns did the same. The Canadian Department of National Defence and the Canadian Forces also banned cosmetic pesticides.

You the man, Jean-Dominic!

Jean-Dominic Leversque-Rene not only won his battle against pesticides, but he also won his battle against cancer. In 2005, Jean-Dominic was 21 years old and cancer free. In a speech to Canada's Committee on Environment and Sustainable Development, he said of his fight with cancer, "I want you to know that something positive came out of my illness. Having cancer was not an enjoyable experience, but this struggle taught me to accept my responsibilities as a member of the community. We can do something to help children. You can make a difference."

PAKISTAN

From Rug Maker to Rescuer

IQBAL MASIH

What do you imagine life being like for the average four-year-old? Whatever you're picturing, it's probably nothing like the life of Iqbal Masih, a boy who lived in Pakistan. When Iqbal was four, his parents borrowed money from the owner of a carpet factory. When they couldn't pay back the loan, the owner of the factory demanded they give him Iqbal instead. This situation is called "bonded labor" and is a form of slavery.

At the factory, Iqbal worked 14 hours a day on a gigantic weaving machine called a loom. All day, every day, Iqbal would run from one side of the loom to the other pushing a piece of wood called a shuttle between high rows of tight thread.

The owner of the carpet factory fed Iqbal Masih just enough so that Iqbal could keep working. When Iqbal refused to work, or if he tried to escape—both of which he did more than most children at the factory—the owner beat him with a stick or hung him by his ankles from the factory ceiling. Iqbal was even punished when he accidentally cut himself on the sharp tools—the owner didn't want anyone to get blood on the rugs.

As you can tell, Iqbal had bigger problems than most four-year-olds. And he lived this way until he was 10. That's 27,720 hours of making carpets, being beaten, and not getting enough to eat. For those six years Iqbal slept chained to the loom so that he couldn't escape.

But then Iqbal started hearing rumors. The other workers in the carpet factory whispered that child slavery was illegal, but the police were afraid of the powerful criminals who ran the carpet factories. The workers also whispered that people outside the factory would help them be free, if only they could escape. But how could the children break through the heavy chains?

It turned out that Iqbal's bad treatment was his ticket to freedom. His arms became so thin that he could slip them right through the cuffs of his chains. He didn't tell anybody.

One night, when clouds covered the moon and the only sound was the rough snoring of the other children in the factory, Iqbal silently slipped out of his cuffs and set them down carefully so they didn't clank on the hard ground. Iqbal tiptoed from loom to loom, but he didn't head toward the locked factory door. If you remember, he had once been hung from the factory ceiling. During that punishment, Iqbal had noticed a high, open window. It was toward that window that he climbed. He hung onto pipes and cracks in the walls to keep from falling.

Can you imagine how Iqbal must have felt as he poked his head out into the cool night air and took a breath free of carpet dust?

After a very hard life, Iqbal's fortunes finally changed. The rumors he had heard in the factory were true. An organization called the Bonded Labor Liberation Front helped child slaves. With the help of the group and its leader, Ehsan Ulla Khan, Iqbal was able to start school in the nearby city of Lahore. In his school cubby, Iqbal kept everything he owned: an illustrated book about Easter and a Teenage Mutant Ninja Turtles mask.

When he was 12, Iqbal started speaking about his experiences and about the children who were still working in the carpet factories. At first, he spoke to small groups in his home city. He told audiences about the world's 250 million child workers, many "bonded laborers," just as he had been.

PAKISTAN
population: 166 million
capital: Islamabad

Bonded laborers, Iqbal explained, are people who can't pay back a loan and go to work for the person they owe. Until they pay off the loan, which sometimes is never, they belong to that person—they are slaves. If a parent doesn't want to be a slave, he or she can send a child instead. This is what had happened to Iqbal.

Soon people outside Lahore, and even outside Pakistan, learned about Iqbal. They asked him to bring his message to Sweden and to the United States. And after hearing Iqbal speak, people in those two countries demanded that Pakistan enforce its child-slavery laws. Iqbal's speeches helped lead to the rescue of over 3,000 children!

Iqbal received awards from the International Labor Organization, Reebok, and ABC TV, which recognized him as the Person of the Week.

When Iqbal was making speeches, many people stopped buying carpets made in Pakistan and the owner of Iqbal's old factory, and many others like him, lost a lot of money. These were dangerous people, and Iqbal knew they didn't like him making speeches. But he didn't think anybody would actually hurt a child, especially one who had been ABC's Person of the Week.

He was wrong.

On April 16, 1995, Iqbal Masih was shot and killed in a small village in Pakistan. He was only 12 years old. The police said it was a random shooting and the murder was never solved. But many people believe Iqbal's murder was an act of revenge by the criminals who lost money when child slaves were freed.

Though Iqbal did his best to end child slave labor, there are still children who are forced to work in slave-like conditions—making silk in India, farming sugar cane in El Salvador, picking cotton in Egypt, as soldiers in Burma, and as housekeepers in Morocco, to name just a few. But there are also people working around the globe to stop child labor. These people remember and honor the Pakistani boy named Iqbal Masih.

KIDS HELPING OTHERS

Hear That?

Pop Art

Early Warning System

Workers Unite!

Sow What You Reap

Ryan's Wells

Hear That?

RYAN PATTERSON

Ryan Patterson sat in a burger joint with his girlfriend, Tiff, thinking about what he would do for the upcoming science fair. After winning last year's contest with a computer-controlled search robot he called "Sleuth-bot," Ryan knew that expectations were high. "What have I seen that I can try to improve? What needs to be done?" thought Ryan.

As he and Tiff were sitting there munching their burgers and fries and talking about the science fair, two women came in and walked up to the cash registers. As they ordered, Ryan noticed that one woman was deaf and the other was her interpreter. He thought it would be a pain in the neck to have to depend on someone else to do your talking for you. And right then his science-fair project hit him: "I thought I could try to develop an electronic method that would make it easier for people to communicate," he said.

Most people might not have known where to start. But Ryan Patterson happened to know a thing or two about electrical engineering. He had been inventing things since he was three years old. When he was six, Ryan had helped his dad rewire the addition to their house. Also, since the third grade Ryan had spent every Saturday playing with electronics in his friend's garage.

His friend happened to be John McConnell, a recently retired particle accelerator physicist at the super high-tech Los Alamos Labs. John McConnell was about as good with technology as anybody on the planet. Ryan spent so much time with John and his wife, Audrey, that they were like a third set of grandparents.

Ryan knew a lot about electronics, but the first step toward creating a sign-language translator had nothing to do with fancy gadgets or gizmos. He had to learn about the deaf community and American Sign Language, known as ASL. After Ryan had gathered information, he made a plan.

ASL uses hand, arm, and facial movements to communicate. Ryan knew he would never be able to translate the symbols that use the whole arm and facial expressions. He decided instead to focus his translator on the letters of the alphabet that ASL users sign with their hands.

Because it would translate the movements of the hand, Ryan chose to make his translator out of a golf glove. Inside the glove, he sewed 10 flexible sensors that would bend with the fingers. (Actually, Audrey McConnell did the sewing.) A user would put a hand inside the glove and form the letters. The sensors would tell the computer what the hand was doing, and the computer would match the hand position with a letter of the alphabet. The letters then would pop up on a screen and the ASL user could quickly and easily spell words. The whole rig consisted of the glove and a small screen, the size of a TV remote control.

Needless to say, Ryan Patterson took first place in the science fair.

In fact, this was not the only prize his sign language translator won. It was also the Grand Award winner in the 2001 Intel International Science and Engineering Fair, and it took first place in the Westinghouse Science and Technology Competition. Prizes are cool, but the most important thing to Ryan was that he was able to improve the lives of others. He said, "If I can make

USA
population: 298 million
capital: Washington, D.C.

an innovative device that could help people out—particularly people with disabilities—I'll feel as though I've made a difference."

Since the invention of the sign-language translator, Ryan has toured the United States demonstrating the machine. On the show *Good Morning America*, the producers asked him to test the translator on the air by signing good morning to host Charlie Gibson. By this time, Ryan had learned to spell using ASL like a pro and his hand was a blur as he signed the message. Do you think it was a mistake when, in front of a national audience, the translator screen spelled T-I-F-F W-I-L-L Y-O-U G-O T-O P-R-O-M W-I-T-H M-E?

Pop Art
JUNICHI ONO

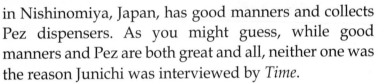

According to *Time* magazine, Junichi Ono, a student at Kurakuen Middle School in Nishinomiya, Japan, has good manners and collects Pez dispensers. As you might guess, while good manners and Pez are both great and all, neither one was the reason Junichi was interviewed by *Time*.

Junichi Ono's teacher said about him, "He will never say or do anything that might hurt someone." But this isn't the reason he was in *Time,* either. One pretty cool thing is that Junichi got to meet Junichiro Koizumi, the prime minister of Japan, and George W. Bush, the 43rd president of the United States.

Junichi remembered George W. Bush as "the guy who choked on a pretzel," and while that may be funny, it's not funny enough to make Junichi famous.

"He's a little strange," said Junichi's classmate.

But being strange doesn't get you a meeting with world leaders and it doesn't get you into *Time* magazine.

When he was six, Junichi's family visited New York City and Junichi drew a picture of the Statue of Liberty. Is that any reason to be featured in *Time* magazine?

Actually, it *is*.

It turns out that Junichi Ono could draw. Not only could he draw — he could draw really, really well! Even as a six-year-old, Junichi was creating drawings that were considered important art. He had his first exhibit in Osaka, Japan, at age eight. "Junichi goes to school," his mother said, "does his homework, plays with his friends — but produces at least 300 drawings a year."

By the time Junichi was 10, he had published his first book of drawings and the Japanese newspapers couldn't get enough of him. The Japan Broadcasting Corporation even made a film about his life. After they televised the film, they had to show it five more times because people kept asking for it.

Junichi showed his art all over Japan and around most of the world — 38 exhibits in all. But he was most excited about his first show in New York City, which was in the winter of 2002. After all, he had loved the city since he first visited with his family when he was six. And it was New York City that had given him the idea for his first famous drawing.

There was one other thing that made Junichi Ono special — in addition to being able to draw really, really well — he also chose to use his art to promote peace in the world and understanding between people.

And nowhere was this more needed than at his show in New York City.

This is because only a few months before Junichi was scheduled to bring his artwork to the city, terrorists crashed two planes into the World Trade Center. The world suddenly seemed like a topsy-turvy place filled with misunderstanding. Some people in the United States mistrusted their neighbors who had come from countries in the Middle East—where the plane hijackers had come from. People got in big arguments over what should be done to stop terrorism. Should we go to war in countries like Iraq and Afghanistan? Some people said yes and some people said no, and nobody could agree on anything.

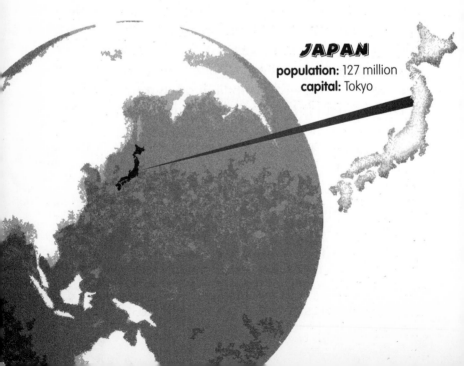

JAPAN
population: 127 million
capital: Tokyo

For a while, it looked like Junichi would have to cancel his show in New York City because of the chaos caused by the disaster. But Junichi, his parents, and the organizers of his exhibit decided that — as they say on Broadway — *the show must go on.*

When Junichi's New York City show opened in February of 2002 — just five months after the disaster — it was obvious that the right decision had been made. Instead of the images of war and destruction that people had seen over and over again since September 11, 2001, Junichi Ono's art showed hope and a world without hate. Visitors to his shows could buy postcards or T-shirts with drawings Junichi had made of New York City. The profits went both to people in Afghanistan and to September 11 disaster survivors.

Junichi Ono showed the world that terror had not triumphed — both New York City and the idea of peace were still alive and well. And in his art, viewers saw what the world should be — what the world could be — if we look past our differences to find the hopes and joys we all share.

Early Warning System

TILLY SMITH

How much do you know about earthquakes and ocean waves? Luckily for more than 100 people on a beach in Thailand, Tilly Smith knew a *whole lot*.

On December 26, 2004, Tilly was vacationing with her family on Maihkao Beach in Phuket, Thailand, when she noticed something strange. "I was on the beach," Tilly remembers, "and the water started to go funny. There were bubbles and the tide went out all of a sudden."

What was happening? Tilly Smith had a good guess.

That's because two weeks earlier, 11-year-old Tilly had studied earthquakes in geography class at her school in Surrey, England. She had loved shaking balsa-wood houses to bits in the earthquake box and seeing whose house could stand the longest. And she also had enjoyed learning about tsunamis, which are giant waves that can be caused when an earthquake shifts the ocean floor. Tilly and her class learned that tsunamis are like the ripples you see when you throw a pebble into a pond, only much, much bigger. They watched a video of the tsunami that struck Hawaii in 1946.

What Tilly saw on Maihkao Beach in Thailand that December morning looked eerily similar to what she had seen in the video. When Tilly looked far out in the water, she noticed that boats on the horizon were bobbing.

Something was coming. And Tilly knew that something would have enough force to rip buildings off their foundations, uproot palm trees as if they were weeds, and scrape the earth clean like a giant lawn mower.

Though it was morning, already more than 100 tourists were lying on the beach on towels and lawn chairs, baking in the sun, and playing in the sand.

"I recognized what was happening and had a feeling there was going to be a tsunami," Tilly said. At first, her mom didn't believe her, but Tilly was persistent. "I was having visions from the Hawaiian videos that I had seen two weeks before," she said. Finally, when the water started to rush out, her mom realized that Tilly was right.

By that time, many of the other people on the beach realized something was up, too—the water didn't usually boil and the tide didn't usually rush out so quickly, leaving boats stranded and fish gasping on the sand. But most people were curious. They stood with their mouths open, watching.

It took Tilly Smith to snap them out of their daze. "Run!" yelled Tilly as she and her mom sprinted up the beach. "I was hysterical," said Tilly, "I was screaming. I said, 'Seriously, there is definitely going to be a tsunami!'"

Tilly and her mom warned security guards who started blowing whistles and waving everyone to higher ground. At first people were confused, and then they were terrified. All of a sudden, the calm beach was in pandemonium. People realized what was about to happen, grabbed their gear, and ran from the water's edge. Behind them the great wave got taller and closer by the second. Now the boats just offshore — the ones that had been left high and dry when the water rushed out — were crushed into splinters as the tsunami smashed into them.

UNITED KINGDOM
population: 61 million
capital: London

Just as the beach was cleared of tourists, the tsunami struck. Tilly and her family watched from the third story of their hotel, which was well back from the water. "Everything went in the swimming pool," recalls Tilly's mom, "beds, palm trees, the lot. Even if you hadn't drowned, you would have been hit by something" if you were on the beach.

It wasn't just the beaches of Thailand that were hit; Indonesia, Malaysia, Bangladesh, India, Sri Lanka, and even Kenya and other parts of East Africa, thousands of miles away, were struck with the massive tidal wave, too. In all, more than 230,000 people were killed.

But the death toll could have been 100 higher if it weren't for Tilly Smith and her knowledge of waves and earthquakes. Not one person was killed or seriously injured on Maihkao Beach. It was one of the only beaches on the east side of Thailand with no deaths.

Workers Unite!
CHEN CHIU-MIAN

When Chen Chiu-Mian was eight years old, her father fell from a painting platform and died. Unfortunately, this was not big news in Taiwan, China, where Chen lived. The death was the painting company's fault—it had given Chen Chiu-Mian's father a faulty safety harness. But this wasn't big news either. In Taiwan, people were hurt on the job every day because of unsafe working conditions. Employers were rarely held responsible for their mistakes. So, again, it wasn't a surprise when the painting company didn't offer to help the family.

What was big news was that Chen Chiu-Mian decided to do something about it. She knew she couldn't take on all the business owners of Taiwan by herself, so she joined the Taiwan Association for Victims of Occupational Injuries (TAVOI). She was ready to change the world, but the first thing she learned at TAVOI was that just because something is unfair does not mean it's easy to fix. And the first step toward fixing workers' rights had nothing to do with going after business owners — at all. First, Chen had to figure out how workers' rights *worked*.

In the United States, businesses have to make sure their employees are safe. For example, if a car factory has old or broken machines that hurt people, the factory owners have to pay the workers' health bills. The owners could also be fined by the government — or shut down if conditions don't improve. Many U.S. workers also belong to groups called *unions*. Unions make sure their members are safe and treated fairly by companies. If a union is unhappy with a business, the workers might walk out and refuse to work until things improve. This is called a strike.

Chen Chiu-Mian didn't need TAVOI to tell her that things in Taiwan were a little different than in the United States. She thought of the owner of her father's painting business. Instead of spending the money to buy her father a working safety harness, the company made him paint from a high platform with little more than his own balance to keep him from falling. As you already know, it wasn't enough.

At TAVOI, Chen found she wasn't the only one with a story of loss. Many others' loved ones had suffered at the hands of greedy business owners. In factories around the country, weak lighting, old equipment, bad ventilation, long hours, and other poor conditions helped the owners make more money. These conditions made working in the factories very unpleasant or downright dangerous.

Why don't the workers just join unions? Chen must have thought. Well, it turns out there were no unions in Taiwan. It's hard to start a union in a place where anybody who complains gets fired and someone who tries to start a union can end up at the bottom of the East China Sea. It was just as difficult in the United States 80 years ago.

Chen Chiu-Mian decided it was time for Taiwan to get up to date.

She started spending all her free time at TAVOI. In addition to learning about workers' rights, Chen also met other people who had lost family members. This made it a little easier to deal with her own loss. "Sometimes after school I was so busy helping out with TAVOI activities that I had to stay up late to finish my schoolwork," she said.

CHINA
population: 1.3 billion
capital: Beijing

Chen Chiu-Mian attended rallies, spoke at TAVOI events, and wrote about the struggles of Taiwan's workers. She also fought to increase respect for the working class. "My mother is a janitor who keeps the park clean," Chen said. "I feel that people consider janitors belong to the lower class." Chen thought it was important for everyone to believe that her mother and others working in nonprofessional jobs were worth as much as doctors and scientists. If they did, it would be harder for business owners to treat janitors, painters, factory workers, and other laborers unfairly.

The press noticed Chen's activism, and in 2004 the *Taipei Times* reported her story as the inspirational article of the week. But still Chen Chiu-Mian felt something was missing. What was missing, of course, was her father.

That's when, Chen recalled, "My mother and I went to a spring ritual in which families could commemorate their loved ones who had passed away." Like in many places around the world, spring in Taiwan meant new flowers and new life after a long winter. And at this spring ritual, after the long winter that was her father's death, Chen finally started to feel warming of her own. And what finally grew in her was the feeling that her father's death had not been in vain. Though her father was gone, Chen would fight on to make sure that other girls' fathers would live.

To this day, Chen Chiu-Mian continues to fight for the rights of Taiwanese workers. The fight is far from over, but Taiwan is now making new laws—and enforcing old ones—to protect its workers.

You may not know it, but you can help Chen's struggle for workers' rights. One way is to buy products only from companies whose goods are manufactured in conditions that are safe and fair for workers.

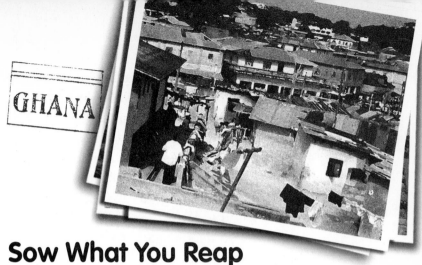

GHANA

Sow What You Reap
P.B.K.L. AGYIREY-KWAKYE

If you were a young person living in Kumikrom in the
Asamonkese District of Ghana, you would spend much
of your time gathering wood. That's because your small,
West African village would not be connected to natural
gas lines or electricity. After your mother filled huge
clay bowls with peeled native vegetables, you would
need to make a fire on which to cook *fufu* — a favorite
dish in Ghana. Every day, you would need to gather
wood for the meal fire.

And every day, you would have to go just a little bit
farther from your village than you did the day before.
Firewood doesn't grow back as fast as you burn it. That
is why Ghana's tropical forest is now only 25 percent of
its original size — the rest of the trees have gone into fire
pits. And the forest continues to shrink by two percent
each year.

If you spend five hours a day — or more! — searching
for enough wood to cook your meals, you miss out on

doing lots of other stuff. There's less time to spend at school learning new things. There is also less time for farming or digging wells. This can make it hard to collect enough food or clean water to survive.

Also, as the forest disappears, the amount of land on which people can grow cocoa shrinks, too. Cocoa is called "black gold" in Ghana because it is the country's largest **cash crop**. Cocoa needs shade to grow. As more trees are cut down for firewood, there is less shade. Less shade means less cocoa, less cocoa means less money, and less money means that people get poorer and poorer every year.

cash crop:
A cash crop is a plant that is grown so that it can be sold to others. Often, cash crops are exported to outside countries to increase a nation's wealth.

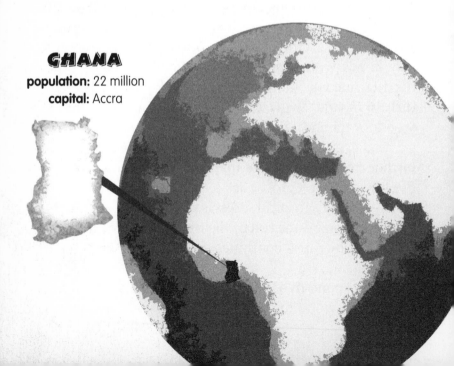

GHANA
population: 22 million
capital: Accra

These reasons are why 14-year-old P.B.K.L. Agyirey-Kwakye decided to plant some trees!

This might seem like the obvious thing to do if there isn't enough firewood or shade, but the villagers of Kumikrom didn't believe it would work.

It takes many years for a tree to grow and we need firewood NOW, they said. *Besides, all the land around our village is already used to grow vegetables. We need these foods to survive – there's no room for trees!*

Also, while the people of Kumikrom knew many tricks for growing food in dry soil, they had no experience growing trees. It just wasn't something that people did. In fact, trees were mostly a pain in the neck— sometimes you had to clear trees so you could plant more crops. So who would ever want to plant them on purpose?

You can't eat a tree, said the people of the village, wisely.

Fortunately, P.B.K.L. Agyirey-Kwakye *did* know how to grow trees. He knew that while you couldn't eat trees, they do have many other uses. Growing up, he had learned about all kinds of trees from his father, who was a forester. If they were out walking, his father would point out different trees—ones that were good for building or that had delicious fruit.

I love chewing on tree branches.

Agyirey-Kwakye's father also told him about eucalyptus trees. Eucalyptus trees grow from seedlings to the size of telephone poles in only three years. And so, on a small piece of land near his house, Agyirey-Kwakye chose to plant eucalyptus for firewood. In the shade between rows of eucalyptus trees, he planted cocoa that could be sold for profit and vegetables that could be eaten. Livestock grazed on the eucalyptus leaves, and the leaves that fell to the ground fertilized the soil.

Later that year, when it was time for harvest, Agyirey-Kwakye's eucalyptus trees had grown tall. His goats were fat and his crops were healthy and ripe. Agyirey-Kwakye sold his cocoa, drank milk from his goats, and used branches from his trees for the fires that cooked the vegetables he had grown. The local farmers were impressed!

The next year P.B.K.L. Agyirey-Kwakye started a group called the Youth Club for Nature Conservation. The club grew 2,000 eucalyptus seedlings, which they gave to 14 local farmers. These farmers were so successful that the next year, 290 new farmers signed up for eucalyptus seedlings, and the club supplied them with 10,000! Once the trees were large enough, some farmers sold them to builders who used them for houses and telephone poles. The farmers used the profits to buy more trees.

And now, instead of walking for miles and miles to get firewood, the young people in the village just chop off a couple of branches on their way home from school.

Ryan's Wells
RYAN HRELJAC

To a six-year-old, $70 is a lot of money.

In 1998, Ryan Hreljac's class in Kemptville, Ontario, was raising money to dig wells in Africa. The teacher explained that although getting water for most Canadians was as easy as turning on the faucet, many children in Uganda had to walk over three miles each way to gather water for their families. Some children walked up to six hours every day to get water, leaving little time for school—not to mention anything fun!

Ryan's teacher explained that even after the kids put in all those hours of work, the water often was unsafe to drink. Many Ugandan children had balloon-shaped bellies from intestinal worms. Nearly one-fourth of the children had diarrhea at any given time, and life-threatening diseases such as typhoid were common. Many children died from drinking unclean water.

The teacher explained to the first-grade class that $70 was enough to drill a new well that could provide water for an entire Ugandan village. Remember, to a six-year-old, that is a lot of money.

Ryan hoped it wouldn't seem like that much money to his parents. When he got home from school that day, he told his mom and dad that he needed $70 for a well in Africa. At first his parents didn't take him seriously, but the next night, Ryan brought it up again. And when his parents refused again, he brought it up one more time the next night.

Finally his parents came to a compromise. "If you're really serious about raising $70," his mom said, "you can do extra chores around the house." She thought that would be the end of it.

CANADA
population: 33 million
capital: Ottawa

But Ryan vacuumed and cleaned and washed windows and picked up pinecones and did all kinds of other chores. After three months of hard work, he had earned $35. You might remember that earning money is not easy when you're six and that's why, *to a six-year-old, $70 is a lot of money*. By now, the school fundraiser was long over, but Ryan was determined to save the money needed for a well. To help him stay motivated, he and his mother drew a large thermometer. They colored it in as Ryan earned more money and got closer to his goal. Ryan's parents wanted him to see that, with hard work, he could make a difference.

When Ryan had *finally* gathered $70 in a cookie tin, he and his parents went to the office of an organization called WaterCan. WaterCan builds wells in developing countries, including Uganda. Ryan presented the money he had earned — $75 in all. He explained that the extra five dollars was to buy lunches for the people digging the well. It seemed like Ryan had accomplished his goal. His parents were happy their son had learned an important lesson and followed through with his plans to help make the world a better place.

The people at WaterCan were happy with Ryan's donation. But they also explained that it actually cost nearly $2,000 to drill a well in Africa, not the $70 Ryan thought. The dollar amount Ryan's teacher had told the class would buy only the small hand pump that sits on top of the finished well, not the well itself.

If you thought $70 was a lot of money to a six-year-old, imagine what $2,000 was like! Many kids might have given up.

Ryan decided to do more chores.

His parents were sad that Ryan would have to learn a difficult lesson — that sometimes even though you try your hardest, some things are still impossible. Remember, it took *months* for Ryan to earn even $70.

But then Ryan's story was published in the local newspaper and his family started getting checks made out to "Ryan's Well." At first the checks came in only a trickle. Then the trickle became a stream and soon the stream became a river. And not long after that, Ryan achieved what his parents thought was impossible. Ryan's well was drilled next to the Angolo Primary School in northern Uganda. Again it looked like he had done his small part for the people of Africa. Now he could say he was finished with the project.

But Ryan wasn't done yet.

Ryan was invited to a WaterCan meeting, where a speaker named Gizaw Shibru told the audience that he would be able to dig more wells in Africa if they had a modern power drill. Unfortunately, Gizaw explained, the drill would cost $25,000. Now, $25,000 is a lot of money to anybody, and it's an especially, mind-bogglingly huge amount of money to a six-year-old.

$25,000?!?

"I'll raise the money for that drill," Ryan said. "I want everybody in Africa to have clean water."

Imagine what his parents must have thought!

But the ball was rolling for Ryan Hreljac. His efforts to raise money for clean water in Africa were featured in newspapers all over North America. He also told people about his cause on TV, including an appearance on *The Oprah Winfrey Show*. Within two months, he had made $7,000 and the donations just kept coming. To date, the Ryan's Well Foundation has raised over $1,500,000 to drill wells in Africa. That's a lot of money to anybody! And more importantly, those wells provide clean water to more than 350,000 people in 10 African countries!

In July of 2000, Ryan got to see his work firsthand. As he drove into the town of Angolo in the back of a truck with his parents and Gizaw Shibru, Ryan could hear the children of the village shouting his name.

"They know my name!" Ryan yelled.

"Everybody for a hundred kilometers knows your name, Ryan," Gizaw said.

When they got to the village, an old man stood up and said, "Look around at our children. You can see they're healthy. This is because of Ryan and our friends in Canada. For us, water is life."

Visit www.ryanswell.ca for more information about Ryan and his charity.

KIDS OVERCOMING CHALLENGES

Back on the Board

A Wish to Breathe Free

The Matchless Girl of Matches

Lemons to Lemonade

New Land, New Life

A Leg Up on the Competition

Back on the Board
BETHANY HAMILTON

Have you ever heard the saying, *When a horse bucks you off, get right back on and ride again?* Have you ever been in a situation like that?

Bethany Hamilton has, but for her the horse was actually a surfboard. And instead of getting bucked off, a 14-foot-long tiger shark bit off her arm.

Bethany was born on the North Shore of Kauai, Hawaii, and started surfing before she could walk. She won her first surfing competition when she was four. At the age of seven she placed first in the 7 to 9 age division in both the short and long board events at the Quicksilver surfing contest. In 2001, she won both the under-14 and under-17 girls divisions of the Volcom Puffer Fish competition. Bethany was sponsored by Rip Curl, a surfboard company, and was making plans to become a professional surfer. She was a surfer girl, born to surfer parents, living in a surfer's paradise. What could be better?

On Halloween morning of 2003, Bethany paddled into the waves of Makua Beach near her home with her best friend, Alana, and Alana's dad and brother. There was nothing unusual about this—in fact, this is how Bethany spent most mornings. Usually her mom and dad were there, too, but Bethany's dad was scheduled for knee surgery that day and was already at the hospital.

The sky was as clear as the water, and the waves were relatively gentle. Bethany surfed for about half an hour and caught maybe 10 waves. Everybody knew each other at Makua Beach, and Bethany, Alana, and about eight other surfers chatted and joked as they straddled their boards in the gentle swells, waiting for the next set of waves to roll in. Bethany dangled her left arm in the water.

USA
population: 298 million
capital: Washington, D.C.

From below, Bethany and her board must have looked like a lazy elephant seal—which many sharks enjoy eating for breakfast.

The tiger shark rose out of the depths and tore into Bethany's board. "We never saw it, or anything, before it bit me," Bethany recalled. "It shook me. It lasted about three seconds long. All I saw was, like, a gray blur. It let go and I just looked at the red blood in the water."

The other surfers pushed Bethany to shore and her friend's dad tied a surfboard leash around what was left of her arm to help slow the bleeding. Alana noted that Bethany stayed "really calm." As Bethany lay on the beach wrapped in towels, she was thinking, *That ambulance should hurry up.*

It was 30 miles to the hospital. When the ambulance arrived there, doctors were preparing Bethany's dad for his knee surgery in the operating room. The doctors quickly went to work on Bethany instead of her father.

Bethany lost 70 percent of her blood. She also lost her left arm, just below the shoulder. Bethany's surgeon said that without her athletic conditioning she probably would have died.

Two weeks later, Bethany and her father both had their stitches removed. Her doctors were sure that the loss of an arm wouldn't hold Bethany back physically, but they warned that getting over the mental and emotional shock of a shark attack would be hard—maybe impossible. Though her wound healed within a month, her friends and family worried that Bethany might never again get back on her surfboard.

Imagine what it must have been like for Bethany Hamilton to sit on her surfboard, only 10 weeks after her injury, waiting to catch that first wave. What do you think was going through her mind? Would you have been afraid if it had been you? Others wanted to give her a push to make sure she could still get up, but Bethany said, "I want to make sure I catch the first wave myself, then they can help me."

Finally a good wave came and Bethany paddled as hard as she could. When she felt the wave start to push her board, she jumped up and planted her feet wide. "When I got up on my first wave," she said, "I just had, like, tears of happiness. . . . I was so stoked to be out there."

But Bethany didn't stop with catching a wave or two. In the same year, she placed fifth in the National Surfing Championships. She competed against professionals with many more years of experience — and both their arms! She also won an ESPN award for Best Comeback Athlete and a special courage award for showing courage at the 2004 Teen Choice Awards. Most importantly to Bethany, she secured a spot on the U.S. Surfing Team. Since her injury and amazing recovery, Bethany has been featured in dozens of newspaper and magazine articles and has appeared on talk shows including *20/20, Good Morning America,* and *The Oprah Winfrey Show.*

How has all the attention changed her?

"People I don't even know come up to me. I guess they see me as a symbol of courage and inspiration. One thing hasn't changed—and that's how I feel when I'm riding a wave. It's like, here I am. I'm still here. It's still me and my board."

Visit www.bethanyhamilton.com for more cool info about Bethany.

A Wish to Breathe Free

IZIDOR RUCKEL

If you're like most people, you probably like doing things outside. Maybe you love biking or skiing or playing team sports like soccer or baseball. Or maybe your thing is catching some sun on the beach, hiking in the woods, or just looking up at stars in the night sky.

Until he was 10 years old, Izidor Ruckel hadn't done any of those things.

In fact, by the time Izidor was 10, he had been outdoors exactly twice—once when his parents dropped him off at an orphanage and once when he was moved to another orphanage—one for older children.

How could it be that at 10 years old Izidor had been outside only twice?

Well, when Izidor was a baby, the disease polio had crippled his leg. In Romania, where he lived, children with disabilities were hidden away from the rest of the world. At the time, Romanian law forced women to have at least five children so that there would be more people to grow up and become workers. Anyone who couldn't work was considered an embarrassment. They were placed in orphanages and adult homes where they could be kept out of sight as cheaply as possible.

In the second orphanage where Izidor lived, there were about 400 other children with disabilities. On cots lined up against the wall, the children slept two to a bed, head-to-toe. If someone wet the bed, it could be weeks before the sheets were changed.

Once, Izidor and another child were caught mimicking one of the orphanage nannies behind her back. In a regular school or childcare, they might have been given detention or a time-out. But in the Romanian orphanage, both boys were beaten with a broomstick until they couldn't move.

"For nine years, I didn't even know what hope was," says Izidor. Many of Izidor's friends died in the orphanage. There was a good chance that he would, too.

But in 1990, Izidor's fortune changed. An American filmmaker visited the orphanage and Izidor's story was shown on the ABC TV program *20/20*. The video caught the eye a Californian couple who was looking to adopt a child. When they saw Izidor on television, they immediately wanted to help him. After a long adoption process, Izidor went to live with the Ruckels in sunny California. When he landed at Los Angeles International Airport, Izidor thought the terminal would be his new home.

Living in the United States was not easy at first. Izidor believed the people in Romania who had told him that his new parents would not love him. When he arrived in Los Angeles, the only thing he could say in English was "no love you!" Luckily, Izidor was wrong about his new parents. They loved their son and wanted to do all they could to care for him. The Ruckels brought Izidor to the Shriners Hospital in San Diego. After six operations, Izidor was able to walk on his leg that had been crippled by polio.

This is an amazing story of survival, but it wasn't enough for Izidor. He realized that he had been given a great chance at a happy life. He knew others back in the Romanian orphanages who were not so lucky. "I have a choice," he said. "I can go on with my life and forget about them, or I can do something about it." Izidor decided to do something about it.

Izidor contacted a group called Cherish Our Children International and asked how he could help.

ROMANIA
population: 22 million
capital: Bucharest

The organization said that orphans in Romania were like dust hidden under a carpet—no one knew about them, so no one helped. Izidor made it his mission to lift up the carpet so that everyone could see them.

When he was 15, Izidor started touring the United States, speaking about the horrible treatment of Romanian orphans. It wasn't hard for him—all he had to do was tell his story. In gyms and lecture halls across the country, he stood squinting into bright spotlights and telling people about the 160,000 kids who still lived in government orphanages. These kids received between two and five minutes of attention per day. He told audiences about the beatings he had received and the hopelessness he had felt. He told people that babies who were born with AIDS, or those who got the disease through unclean blood transfusions, were abandoned in the streets. And he told people how they could help.

Izidor put a face on the Romanian orphan crisis. In the 1990s, aid from all over the world started pouring into the country. People also began adopting children from the orphanages. Today there are hundreds of organizations dedicated to helping Romanian children.

Nice work, Izidor!

Izidor ended his speeches around the United States by saying, "no one must ever forget."

Izidor did not give these words only as a promise, he lived them. In 2001, Izidor went back to Romania on a trip sponsored by ABC TV. He said of his visit, "I went back to the hospital where I had been kept for 11 years. I saw many friends there, friends I grew up with, still in the same hospital, living under the same terrible conditions I'd left 10 years before. It nearly broke my heart." But living in the United States, what else could Izidor do for them?

He decided the answer was *not enough*. On November 28, 2005, Izidor moved back to Romania for good. He said about his continuing work with Romanian orphans, "I am hoping that I can start new projects, since I will be on hand to see what is needed." Already he has succeeded in making sure his Romanian friends are not forgotten.

You can read about Izidor in his book *Abandoned for Life*. To learn about things you can do to help children in need around the world, visit www.cherishourchildren.org.

The Matchless Girl of Matches
FATEMA BEGUM

Growing up in Bangladesh, Fatema Begum was the eldest of nine children. Can you imagine what her one-room, tin-roof house sounded like? At any time there were kids of all ages running in and out, crying and eating, talking and playing, and getting into mischief and everything else that nine kids could possibly do.

Sometimes it was all her mom could do to keep the house from dissolving into total chaos! And sometimes it was all Fatema's father could do to feed his family of 11. In fact, the money he earned by selling goods on the street never seemed like enough. Much of the time, the Begum children went to bed hungry.

The family needed help and because Fatema was the eldest, it was up to her. To support the family, Fatema worked in a match factory. The hours at the factory were long and the working conditions were poor. And as you might imagine, making matches was a very dangerous job. But without the money Fatema earned, the family might not survive.

Unfortunately, Fatema was not alone in her tough situation. In Bangladesh, 700,000 kids under the age of 15 work in factories. The factories like to hire children because they can pay them less and because children are less likely to fight back against bad working conditions.

Fatema and her family lived next to the match factory with the other workers who couldn't afford to take the bus from farther away. The neighborhood was a ramshackle patchwork of small, poorly built houses. Every morning when Fatema woke up, she would slide off the cot she shared with two of her siblings. She would walk through the rows of homes to the shared bathroom, then go in search of clean water. As the sun came up, she would be off to work in the factory.

Most people who worked in the match factory worked there until they died. Without an education, what else could they do? But Fatema Begum was not most people and she had another life in mind. But she couldn't quit her job at the factory or her parents and younger brothers and sisters would have even harder lives.

Fatema found an opportunity when the Underprivileged Children's Educational Program opened a school in Char Chakti, the neighborhood where she lived. The school didn't charge money for tuition. And students could attend for only a few hours per day — so Fatema could keep her job at the match factory *and* go to classes.

At first Fatema's parents didn't think it was such a good idea. They loved her and wanted her to follow her dreams, but they worried she would lose her job. *What if school interfered with work and Fatema couldn't do a good job at the match factory? If she was fired,* her parents worried, *the family might starve.* They didn't want to risk not being able to provide for their other eight children so that Fatema could go to school.

Please! Fatema must have begged. *I know I can do it. I know I can earn money while going to school.*

Finally her parents gave in—Fatema could go to school if it didn't affect her job. Working during the day and studying at night, Fatema finished the eighth grade at age 15. Unfortunately, at that time the school didn't offer high school courses. With only an eighth-grade education, Fatema still couldn't find a job outside the match factory. Despite all her hard work, it looked like Fatema would still be stuck.

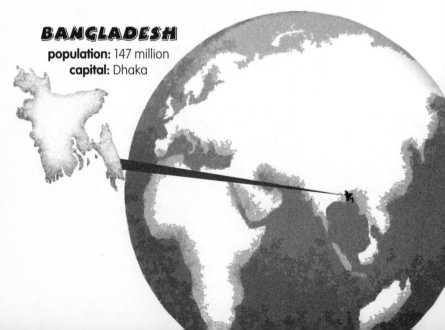

BANGLADESH

population: 147 million
capital: Dhaka

It wasn't until an aid organization sponsored a three-month tailoring school in Char Chakti that Fatema's luck changed again. She begged and pleaded with her parents once more, and finally they allowed her to attend sewing classes in the evenings. She also started a small business, raising chickens to sell out of her family's one-room house.

Do you ever feel tired after school? Like you want to take a long nap? Imagine working an entire job *before* going to school. This is what Fatema did every day and it wasn't easy. Work and school and chickens and helping out her family left her with only a couple hours for sleep each night.

But Fatema stuck with it and finished the tailoring course. By this time, she was 16 years old and had spent almost 10 years working in the match factory. Fatema used the little money she had saved from her chicken business to buy a sewing machine and advertised her services as a tailor.

At first, Fatema only got a few clothing orders. But she knew that sewing was her chance to escape the match factory, and so she put her heart into every project. And with each item she sewed, Fatema got a little better and a little faster. As her reputation spread around the neighborhood, the orders increased. She saved more and more money and finally the day came when Fatema was able to walk out of the match factory for the final time!

Not only did the money from Fatema's sewing business help support the family, but it also helped pay for her to go back to school—this time to be a teacher. Fatema is now an adult-education instructor and trainer for World Vision's Health and Development Program. She has also started a coaching center where the children of Char Chakti can learn to read and write. Children who work in the factories can attend Fatema's coaching center for free, whenever they like, and improve their lives through learning—which happens to be something Fatema knows a little bit about.

Lemons to Lemonade

ALEXANDRA SCOTT

Maybe you've heard the expression, *When life gives you lemons, make lemonade.* It means taking a bad situation and making something good out of it.

Alexandra Scott knew a little bit about doing this.

Her "lemon" was neuroblastoma—a deadly form of childhood cancer. And her "lemonade" was, well... lemonade. Alex had been battling neuroblastoma since before her first birthday. When she was four, she opened a lemonade stand on her corner to help fight the disease.

What? A lemonade stand? How can a lemonade stand help fight cancer? Maybe it's because cancer doctors like lemonade? Maybe drinking sour lemonade makes doctors' brains work better? Actually, Alex started a lemonade stand to help doctors pay for cancer research. She knew that every little bit helps, and she thought maybe—*just maybe*—she could make a difference.

Some people thought Alex was wasting her time. After all, what difference could 50 cents here and 50 cents there make when cancer research costs millions of dollars?

Alex didn't worry about this. Instead, she and her brother, Patrick, lugged a table out to the front yard. They made a sign that said *Alex's Lemonade Stand for Pediatric Cancer – 50 Cents a Glass*, and taped it to the front of the table. Then they sat, side by side, at the table, pouring lemonade and dropping the nickels, dimes, and quarters into a tin can for safekeeping.

Alex worked at her lemonade stand whenever she could. Sometimes the stand was so busy that her dog, Shammy, had to help. Sometimes business was so slow that she sat around reading.

And some days were easier than others. Remember, Alex wasn't just fighting against childhood cancer in general, she was fighting *her own* cancer, too. The

USA
population: 298 million
capital: Washington, D.C.

chemotherapy and radiation—treatments for cancer patients—made her hair fall out and made her so sick that it was hard to get out of bed. "Alex would have died many years ago if there hadn't been newer, experimental therapies," said her doctor. And it was research for these new treatments that Alex was raising money to help scientists discover.

Over the summer, Alex raised $2,000. That's 4,000 cups of lemonade—or about 40 cups of lemonade every day for three months! To be fair, some people who stopped by Alex's stand didn't come for the lemonade. As the word of Alex's lemonade spread, some people just stopped by to drop a dollar or two into the tin can. At the end of the summer, Alex donated the money and closed the stand—nobody wants lemonade in the winter!

That winter her family moved to Philadelphia, where Alex could get specialized treatment for her cancer. She missed her old neighborhood—and her lemonade stand.

But moving wasn't all bad for Alex. At the Children's Hospital of Philadelphia she met many new friends. Alex thought it was great to finally have people she could talk to about her cancer. Her friends understood her because they were going through the same thing. But it was also hard. That year, one of Alex's new friends, Toireasa, died of neuroblastoma. One day Toireasa was there and the next day she was not. It wasn't fair.

Alex did the thing she knew how to do best—she set up a lemonade stand in honor of Toireasa. It was a new stand in a new neighborhood, and Alex didn't know if anyone would actually show up. But, her mom said, "She's determined about anything that's important to her, whether it's what kind of ice cream she's eating or raising money." Alex sat at her stand day after day. Soon her determination paid off—people started lining up for lemonade! Some took a cup and some just donated money. That year, she raised $18,000.

Alex appeared on *The Oprah Winfrey Show* and the *Today* show as well as in *People, Time,* and *USA Today.* Kids around the country started to think of lemonade stands as more than a way to make a little extra money for music downloads or video games—many of these kids opened their own "Alex's Lemonade" stands and donated the money to cancer research.

The next year—despite pouring rain—Alex earned $40,000 in three hours. She had gone from having people drop change in her tin can to people packing in dollar bills and donating checks made out to "Alex's Lemonade." Kids who opened stands around the country earned another $220,000.

Alex was *still* thinking bigger—her goal was to raise $1 million for child cancer research.

But this whole time, Alex's own cancer was getting worse. Before opening the fifth annual lemonade stand, her mother said, "She's tired. She's exhausted. Her future has always been uncertain, but I don't think any of us—me, my husband, her doctor—has felt this pessimistic before." Her parents wanted Alex to cut back on the energy she put into raising money, but Alex wouldn't miss a chance to appear on the *Today* show to publicize her lemonade stands. In this fifth year of the event, more than 1,000 stands sprang up around the country, raising close to $1.5 million.

Unfortunately, Alex was not to see the sixth year.

On August 1, 2004, Alex passed away peacefully in her sleep. "She just slipped away," her mom said. "You could see when she was ready. She let off a big sigh, and went off to sleep. She was very calm. For that, we're grateful." Alex was eight years old.

When Alex and her brother first hauled a table out to their front yard, do you think anyone imagined how big the lemonade project would get?

In fact, the idea became so big that even though Alex is gone, her stands are still going strong. Every year people — from preschoolers to senior citizens — gather cups, chairs, a sign, and a pitcher and sell lemonade in Alex's memory. Though these groups are happy to help, they always hope that maybe next year they won't need to open a lemonade stand. Maybe someday there will be a cure for childhood cancer. Because of Alexandra Scott's help, that day may come soon.

For more information about Alexandra Scott or to find out how you can open an Alex's Lemonade stand, visit www.alexslemonade.org.

ETHIOPIA

New Land, a New Life
MAWI ASGEDOM

Do you sometimes wonder if you *actually* remember something or if you just remember your family *telling* you about it? Isn't that weird?

Here's what Mawi Asgedom says about *his* earliest memories:

"The desert, I remember. The shrieking hyenas, I remember. But beyond that, I cannot separate what I remember from what I have heard in stories. . . . I remember playing soccer with rocks, and a strange man telling me and my brother, Tewolde, that we had to go on a trip."

The man was warning them of the approaching Ethiopian army. If they didn't leave their village quickly, they would be killed. And Mawi and his family didn't get to drive in a dune buggy or take a train—they had to cross the desert on foot. Mawi was three years old.

Mawi, his mother, and Tewolde walked toward the country of Sudan, where the boys' father was waiting and where they hoped to find safety. Unfortunately, when they finally reached Sudan, they found it was no place to escape war. Rebels were fighting the government and there was even violence in the refugee camp itself. Boys used sticks and rocks to fight each other for food.

To Mawi's mother and father, this was no way to raise children. They wanted peace and they wanted their children to have a chance at a better life. They wanted to go to a place called *America*.

An organization called World Relief helped the family enter their name in a lottery for permission to come to the United States. After a long wait, their chance came.

One day Mawi was in a refugee camp in Sudan. The next day he boarded an airplane for the first time. And the day after that he was in a hotel room in Chicago, in America at last. Outside the room, cars whizzed past honking their horns. Lights flashed green and yellow and red, and pavement and huge buildings were everywhere. Do you know the dizzy feeling you get when you look down from a bridge or the high branches of a tree? Mawi quickly found out you can get this same feeling looking up. Try it sometime! When Mawi craned his neck back to look at the skyscrapers, he almost fell over backward.

For the first two weeks in America, the only time the family left the hotel room was with a volunteer from World Relief. "We yearned for a piece of *injera* bread," Mawi remembers, "or a bowl of *sebhi* stew." Think of all the things you might miss about home if you suddenly had to move to another country.

And from the first day in Chicago, Mawi remembers his father telling him and his brother, "Right now we are among the poorest in the land. Neither your mother nor I will find good work because we lack schooling. We will have to work backbreaking jobs, we will never fully understand our rights, and others will take advantage of us. But if you, our children, work hard at school and finish the university, maybe someday you can help yourselves and help your family, too."

To Mawi's father, education was the solution for a better life.

But war was not yet done with Mawi. It followed him to the playground at elementary school in Wheaton, Illinois. Other kids called Mawi and Tewolde names and teased them about the starving people in the boys' homeland of Ethiopia. Mawi and Tewolde responded by

ETHIOPIA
population: 75 million
capital: Addis Ababa

fighting. These fights continued until their father said, "Let them hit you. Come home beaten and bruised. Do not ever fight back." Mawi and Tewold couldn't believe it! Weren't they right to stand up against this name-calling and abuse?

But their father was afraid that if the brothers kept fighting, they would be expelled from school. And then how would they get scholarships to attend university? He explained that fists were not the only tools for fighting and that sometimes *not fighting* took more bravery. Mawi and his brother tried to be brave.

In middle school, Mawi had to be especially brave. Tewolde, halfway through his senior year in high school, was killed by a drunk driver.

Mawi had been getting Ds in most of his classes. But when his brother was killed, something inside Mawi changed. He knew there had to be a reason that he was still alive. All of a sudden life seemed so precious—like he had to make the most of every moment.

Congratulations, Mawi!

In high school, Mawi worked hard. He read and studied and dreamed of getting a scholarship to a good college. Mawi wanted to make his brother proud. The more he thought about it, the more he also wanted to succeed for himself. Through his hard work, he received A's in high school. When he graduated, not only did he get into college, he earned a full scholarship to Harvard University!

In 1999, Mawi spoke at his Harvard graduation ceremony. But his father was not there to hear the speech. Like Tewolde, Mawi's father had also been killed by a drunk driver.

After earning his degree from Harvard, Mawi decided he wanted to help others. Instead of taking a job in business or technology like many of his friends did, Mawi started speaking to audiences around the United States. He told his story and inspired teens to find their own power and success. He also wrote a book about his experiences. "There are certain people who really inspired me, such as my father and brother," Mawi said. "I thought that others could benefit from hearing about them, too."

For more information about Mawi Asgedom, visit www.mawispeaks.com or read his book, *Of Beetles and Angels.*

A Leg Up on the Competition

RUDY GARCIA-TOLSON

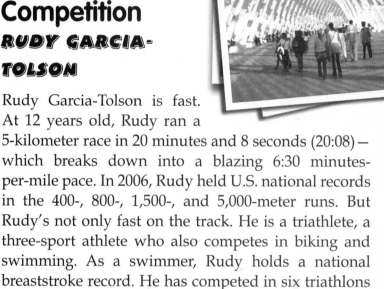

Rudy Garcia-Tolson is fast. At 12 years old, Rudy ran a 5-kilometer race in 20 minutes and 8 seconds (20:08) — which breaks down into a blazing 6:30 minutes-per-mile pace. In 2006, Rudy held U.S. national records in the 400-, 800-, 1,500-, and 5,000-meter runs. But Rudy's not only fast on the track. He is a triathlete, a three-sport athlete who also competes in biking and swimming. As a swimmer, Rudy holds a national breaststroke record. He has competed in six triathlons and looks forward to entering an Ironman competition someday, which includes a 2.4-mile swim, a 112-mile bike ride, and a 26.2-mile run.

There's one other pretty amazing thing about Rudy: He doesn't have legs.

Rudy was born with pterygium syndrome. Webs of skin behind his knees connected his upper and lower leg—kind of like a tight version of the skin between your thumb and first finger. This skin kept his legs bent and made it impossible for him to walk. By the time Rudy was five, he had undergone 15 surgeries but still couldn't stand out of a wheelchair. "I was born with a birth defect," Rudy said. "The doctors gave me and my family a choice: Cut off my legs or stay in a wheelchair. I told the doctors to cut my legs off."

As you can imagine, it wasn't easy losing both legs from the knee down. "When he went back to kindergarten, he was a little bit down," Rudy's mom recalled. "The school counselor recommended putting him in a sport and his dad suggested swimming." It wasn't long after that Rudy set the goal of competing in the **Paralympic Games**. But he knew it would take years of hard work. In elementary school, Rudy started training in the pool five days a week in two-hour sessions. He learned to run and bike as well. Don't let his easy smile and casual charm fool you—Rudy is a serious athlete!

Paralympic Games:

The Paralympic Games are held every four years and feature athletes with disabilities competing in many sports.

But Rudy's life wasn't all about training. His mom made sure that he found time to be a good student. "He knows he can't go to swim practice or to any of the speaking engagements he loves so much if his grades aren't good," his mom said. His family also made sure Rudy had at least one weekend a month free just to be a kid. After all, while Rudy may have been one of the best Para athletes in the world by the time he was a middle schooler, he was still just a regular kid. Rudy hung out with friends, listened to cool music, played paintball, and dyed his hair platinum blond.

But unlike most other middle schoolers, one corner of Rudy's living room in Bloomington, California, was completely full of prosthetic legs. There were light, springy pairs for running; pairs with hinged knees and clips for bike pedals; and durable, stable pairs, called stubbies, for walking, playing paintball, and skateboarding. Have you ever heard somebody talk about how hard it is to walk in high-heeled shoes? Imagine what it's like getting used to different legs—and Rudy even switched from swimming legs to biking legs to running legs in the middle of races!

But despite his legs that ended at the knee, Rudy hated the term *disabled* and rejected *handicapped*. How could you call him handicapped when he was the one winning paintball every weekend?

It was five days after his 15th birthday when Rudy walked into the Aquatic Center in Athens, Greece, for the finals of the 200-meter individual medley swimming race at the 2004 Paralympics. More than 1 million people watched the games. There were 50 broadcasters and 3,000 reporters from all over the world covering the events.

USA
population: 298 million
capital: Washington, D.C.

Rudy Garcia-Tolson was the youngest member of the U.S. Paralympics team in Athens. To win the 200-meter individual medley, swimmers have to be experts in the backstroke, breaststroke, butterfly, and freestyle. It was an especially difficult race for Rudy because the breast-stroke is almost completely leg-powered. But that hadn't stopped him from shattering the world record by 3.42 seconds in a qualifying round.

When the bell for the 200-meter individual medley final sounded, Rudy launched into the pool and carved through the water with his powerful arms. He tried to swim his own race without worrying about the competition. Coming down the homestretch, he knew he was fast—but just how fast, he didn't know. Rudy reached out his fingers, touched the wall, and looked up.

He had won the gold medal! In his first Paralympics, Rudy had beaten the best swimmers in the world! For his performance, ESPN nominated Rudy as one of the three most outstanding Para athletes of 2004.

Victory!

Paul Martin, one of the world's top disabled athletes, said, "He has already done wonders for challenged athletes and he's just a kid. I look forward to the day he kicks my butt in a triathlon. He already kicks it in the water."

While Rudy has trained his arms and lungs to be amazingly strong, he doesn't credit his success to that. Instead, Rudy Garcia-Tolson says he has a different secret weapon: "A brave heart is a powerful weapon."

KIDS USING TALENTS & CREATIVITY

See It to Believe It

Outta This World

Sports Hero

Beyond His Years

Young Master Yani

Snail Paint

See It to Believe It

KRUTI PAREKH

Thirteen-year-old Kruti Parekh stood on a stage in her hometown of Mumbai, India, eating newspaper in front of a cheering crowd. She packed her cheeks until she looked like a deranged chipmunk, but the crowd kept yelling and Kruti kept packing in the paper. Finally, Kruti raised her right hand and the crowd fell silent. With a dramatic flair, Kruti inserted her thumb and forefinger into her mouth to pulled out the wad of chewed-up newspaper. But instead of a gross ball of paper, out came a long string of colored ribbon. Kruti, the human recycling machine, had turned old newspaper into yards and yards of brand-new ribbon! "You see," Kruti yelled to the crowd, "if we discard paper in the right place, we can recycle it and use it again!"

Next Kruti threw an old banana peel into an empty box. "Sim Silabi Fu Fu Fu!" she cried. These are her magic words, which mean "this will drive you crazy, crazy, crazy!" After she waved her wand, bouquets of roses burst from the box.

Kruti could also eat fire and razor blades, drink acid, walk on fire, bathe with burning coals, pull an airplane with her teeth, levitate her friends, and sleep on a bed of sharp arrows while having cement blocks on her chest broken with a hammer.

At 13, Kruti was India's youngest female magician. "I got interested in magic when I was five," Kruti said. "I saw a magician doing tricks for a crowd by the roadside. I was hypnotized by his tricks and decided to learn magic myself." Kruti used her magic to spread the message of environmental conservation. She would tell her audiences that if they separated their trash, 85 percent could be reused. "The organic waste" — leftover food, for example — "can be composted into fertilizer. We can then use it to grow fruits and vegetables without chemicals." Then, Kruti said, the nonorganic trash — like paper, glass, and metal — could be recycled. Of the remaining 15 percent of waste, "8 percent is plastic bags," she continued, "and we can get rid of them by using cloth bags when we shop. It's only the remaining 7 percent that we can't do anything about. So we can reduce the trash heap from 100 to 7 percent! Sim Silabi Fu Fu Fu!"

Kruti knew that lectures about the environment could be pretty boring, but she hoped that by mixing environmentalism and magic she would be able to reach kids who otherwise might not care.

In addition to performing magic, Kruti Parekh founded the Eco-Kids Club, where children in Mumbai could learn about environmental causes such as composting and vermiculture, which is using worms to turn trash into fertilizer. With the Eco-Kids Club, Kruti was able to get over 100 schools to participate in conservation and recycling efforts.

But Kruti's environmental activism didn't stop with just educating people about environmental conservation.

Every month, worshipers at the Hindu temple in the city of Mumbai bring more than a ton of fresh flowers to the temple. It used to be that when the flowers wilted, they were thrown into the ocean. But Kruti worked with the temple to set up a composting system that turned flower waste into fertilizer. Now the temple uses the dead flowers to help grow new flowers, showing the cycle of birth, death, and rebirth that is part of the Hindu religion.

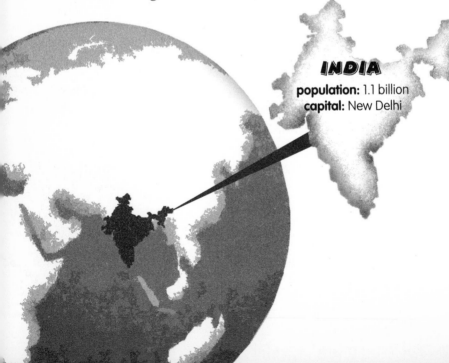

INDIA
population: 1.1 billion
capital: New Delhi

Kruti and her eco-club also adopted the Charni Road Train Station, which had always been notoriously filthy and gross. The club installed trash bins and painted the train station walls with murals showing a clean environment. Today the Charni Road Train Station is one of the cleanest in Mumbai.

In India, a 13-year-old female magician who promoted saving the environment was not something you would find on any old street corner. Kruti Parekh quickly became famous for her message of magic. She performed all over the world. In 1996 she toured Africa and donated the money she made to the Feed the Babies fund. As of 2005, she had performed more than 3,000 shows and had entertained and educated presidents, kings, queens, sheiks, and maharajahs.

By the time she was 16, Kruti's fame allowed her to adopt Sharda Mandir High School in Mumbai. She helped provide teacher salaries, lunches, uniforms, and busing to more than 1,000 kids from families in need. Of course, the school is also eco-friendly.

Sim Silabi
Fu Fu Fu!

Outta This World

CHRISTOPHER PAOLINI

Can you imagine setting off on an adventure to explore the world? What would you pack? How would you travel? Who would you bring along? Christopher Paolini packed a sword and brought his best friend — an electric-blue dragon, named Saphira.

Growing up in Montana's Paradise Valley, Christopher read fantasy stories like *Lord of the Rings* and *Dragonsong*. And looking out his window he saw mythical adventure waiting. He took long hikes with his family through the jagged Absaroka and Beartooth mountains and among the bubbling mud-pots of Yellowstone National Park. He heard wolves howling at night and watched migrations of elk pass through the valley. He could almost feel the wind of leathery dragon wings soaring over the craggy ridges and whistling low through the treetops.

Christopher was homeschooled and completed high school at only 15 years old. Instead of going to college right away, he decided to wait until he was the same age as other college freshmen.

He thought about what he might do in the few years before he turned 18 and decided to write a book.

Actually, he decided to write a series of three books about a world he invented called *Alagaësia*. First he sat down and wrote a quick summary of what would happen in all three books. Then he got to work. He was so excited that he wrote the first 60 pages with a pen and paper — "until I learned how to type," he said. Christopher invented his own world, his own characters, his own plot, and even three of his own languages, which he based on Old Norse — the ancient language of the vikings.

And he mashed all this invention together with things he saw every day. In an interview, Christopher said, "Oftentimes when I'm in the forest or in the mountains, sitting down and seeing some of those little details makes the difference between having an okay description and having a unique description. For instance, maybe there's moss there, but maybe I know from personal experience that the moss feels like mouse fur when it's being petted." Christopher even put details from his own life into his book — including his sister. "Fortunately for my bodily well-being," Christopher wrote, "she has an excellent sense of humor."

By the end of 1999, Christopher thought he had finished his book *Eragon*, but he soon discovered the real work had just begun. When he reread the book he thought it was too long. He also felt the action was too slow and the writing was "mired in atrocious language and grammar" — in other words, not very good.

This is the point where many authors might give up on a project. But Christopher did no such thing. Instead, he spent almost an entire year revising *Eragon*. When he completed his second draft he felt it was "bloated with far too many words." There was *still* a lot of work left to be done.

He spent *another* full year revising the book again. Imagine writing thousands and thousands of words and

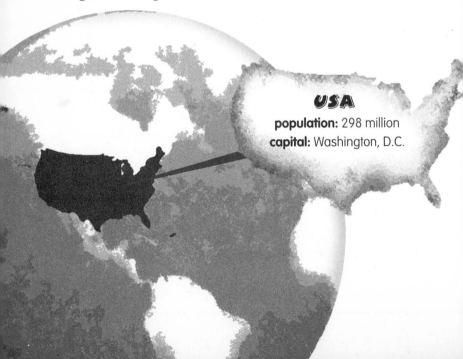

USA
population: 298 million
capital: Washington, D.C.

then deleting most of them! But Christopher believed in his project and kept working. With the help of his parents, both published authors, Christopher was able to "quicken the pace of the story so that *Eragon* read the way that I had intended it to."

So, once you have a book, publishers will beat down your door trying to get you to publish it, right? Uh . . . not exactly. Even after Christopher Paolini had finished *Eragon*, revised it, and polished it again until it sparkled like dragon scales, he still had to find a way to get the book into the hands of readers. He and his family decided to self-publish the book. Christopher drew his own cover, designed his own maps of Alagaësia, and sent the book away to be printed. He paid for everything with his own money.

And then, even after he had a crate of books sitting on his doorstep, Christopher somehow had to sell those books to stores and readers. To get people interested, Christopher presented his book to groups wherever he could. He read from the book at bookstores, libraries, and schools in Livingston, Bozeman, and Billings, and at book fairs all over the country. He even remembers arm-wrestling a young man to get him to read *Eragon*. "Fortunately I won!" remembered Christopher.

It was at the Northwest Bookfest in Seattle, Washington, that Christopher talked with an editor from the publishing house called Knopf. They wanted to publish his book! All this was icing on the cake for Christopher, who had started *Eragon* for the love of writing and "to feel a sense of magic in the world."

Eragon and Christopher's super-successful sequel, *Eldest*, have both landed on bestseller lists everywhere. And today, most people think of Christopher Paolini as a mega-famous author. But they don't realize that he started as a young person with only an idea, a pen, and a notebook full of blank paper—just like you!

You can find *Eragon* and *Eldest* at most libraries and bookstores. Check them out for a fantastic journey to a new world!

VIETNAM

Sports Hero

NGUYEN NGOC TRUONG SON

In 2004, Nguyen Ngoc Truong Son was named Athlete of the Year in Vietnam without ever breaking a sweat. Other athletes lower on the list included Nguyen Duy Bang, who cleared 2.25 meters to break the Southeast Asian high-jump record, and Do Ngan Thuong, who won three gold medals at the Malaysian Gymnastics Championships.

At the time he was named Athlete of the Year, Nguyen Ngoc Truong Son was only 14 years old. He played chess—which is considered one of Vietnam's most important "sports."

"I just see things on the board and know what to do," Son said. "It's just always made sense to me."

Son's parents were teachers in the province of Kien Giang, which is in the Mekong Delta region of Vietnam. After a long day of teaching, they often played chess on a board Son's father had made from plywood and a felt-tipped pen. When Son was three years old, he watched over his mother's shoulder as she moved the pawns, rooks, bishops, knights, queen, and king around the board. He noticed there was a certain way that each of the funny-shaped pieces could move, and he laughed when his mother or father knocked over each other's pieces.

It looked like fun and soon Son wanted to play, too. He pestered his parents to let him try. Finally his parents gave in, thinking three-year-old Son would try to eat the pieces or pretend to chase the bishops around with the knights. To their surprise, Son set up the board correctly and knew how the pieces moved. Within a month he was beating his parents.

"It's an inborn gift," said his father. "You couldn't train an ordinary three-year-old to play like that." Of course, his father had to say this so that he didn't feel bad about getting beat by a preschooler.

By the time Son was four, he was competing in national chess tournaments. At age seven, he was winning them. Son's parents knew that his skills were special. At one of the tournaments, Son met Trinh Hoang Cuong, who was a chess coach for the province sports department. Cuong remembered, "When I played him a few times, I found that his way of playing was very creative. Son found his own direction in the game and his method brought about the same result—checkmate."

Coach Cuong accepted Son as a student. Together they traveled the country playing tournaments. When he was seven, Son won a silver medal at Vietnam's under-nine National Chess Championship and was invited to play at the World Junior Chess Champion-ship in Greece. Son's parents couldn't travel with him and they worried about him when he was gone. But his father hoped that traveling would bring Son "more experiences and confidence in life."

Son certainly opened his gold-medal match in Greece confidently, using a move where he pushed his bishop's pawn two spaces forward—the *English Opening*. Son knew that he had to control the middle of the board, but he decided to be tricky about it. And the English Open-ing matched his style—it would allow Son to think on his feet and slice in toward the middle of the board once he had taken control of the sides.

His opponent matched the opening, pushing his own bishop's pawn directly in front of Son's. Next Son took a chance—he used a move called the *Queen's Gambit*, sacri-ficing his pawn to draw his opponent's pieces out away

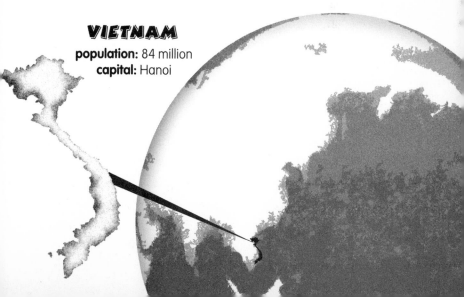

VIETNAM
population: 84 million
capital: Hanoi

from the important center. His opponent accepted the Gambit and it was *game on*. Son hated to sit still during a match. He stood up and walked around, thinking and watching his opponent's eyes.

Move after move, Son used his pawns to tempt his opponent away from the center, the whole time pacing around the board, concentrating on what might happen five, six, seven moves out. And then he attacked, diving into the center of the board with everything he had and making it impossible for his opponent to move anywhere without losing pieces or opening up holes in his defense. His opponent knew he was a goner and lay down his king.

Son had won the gold medal! He later proved his performance in Greece wasn't a fluke. He won the Asian under-14 and under-16 championships as well as the World Junior Chess Championship.

Still, Son had other goals. He was good for an eight-year-old, but how good was he compared to adults? To find out, Son traveled to Hungary, a European country thousands of miles away from home. Here was the home of Chesscom, a school where the best chess players in the world go to sharpen their skills. Son hoped that someday he would be named a chess grandmaster, the highest rank that a person can get.

Someday came sooner than anyone could have guessed. At the age of 14,

Checkmate!

Son became only the second player to be named a chess grandmaster before age 15. Coach Cuong called it "the best achievement in the history of Vietnam's chess players."

Son continues to play—and beat—the world's best chess players. The next goal for Son: being named one of the top 100 chess grandmasters in the world. He's come a long way from beating his parents on a plywood board. And adult chess masters everywhere should know that Son is here to stay. He'll be beating them next!

Beyond His Years
MATTIE STEPANEK

Mattie Stepanek liked barbecue ribs, chocolate ice cream, and seafood. His favorite animal was the tiger. His favorite music was mostly from soundtracks like *Pirates of the Caribbean* and *Lord of the Rings*. He had a pet golden retriever named Micah, who used to steal Mattie's socks and run away wagging his tail. Mattie liked watching *The Simpsons*, going to Starbucks, and, most of all, writing poetry.

If you have ever written poetry, then you know how hard it can be to get the words just right. But Mattie Stepanek wrote poems the way some people might dribble a basketball—he was a natural! In all, he wrote six books filled with poems, which he titled *Heartsongs*, *Hope Through Heartsongs*, *Celebrate Through Heartsongs*, *Loving Through Heartsongs*, *Journey Through Heartsongs*, and *Just Peace*. Even poets who write their entire lives have an almost impossible time putting out books that make the bestseller list. But *all* of Mattie's books made the list—and he wrote them all before he turned 14! To Mattie, writing poetry was as easy as breathing.

In fact, sometimes writing poetry was easier than breathing.

This is because Mattie had a rare form of muscular dystrophy. He described his illness, saying, "My automatic systems, like breathing, heart rate, digestion, and things like that, don't always work well on their own." Can you imagine what it would be like to have to remember to take a breath? Also your heart beats faster when you're running around. But Mattie's heart didn't know when to speed up and slow down. And sometimes it would forget to beat at all. Because of this, Mattie had machines that told his body what to do. He slept with a ventilator that breathed for him—a wire attached to his heart told it when to beat. He wrote all his poems from a motorized wheelchair. When his fingers bled due to poor oxygen circulation and he couldn't write, he spoke his poems into a tape recorder. "One day I will get one of those computer programs that recognizes my voice," he said.

You might think that Mattie would feel cheated by life and that he would choose to write mostly about sad things. Instead, Mattie looked past his illness and chose to write about *heartsongs*. "Your heartsong," Mattie said, "is your inner beauty. It's the song in your heart that wants you to help make yourself a better person, and to help other people do the same. Everybody has one."

In each of his books, Mattie used heartsongs to spread the messages of peace, kindness, goodwill, and optimism. Though he knew he was very, very sick, Mattie always had a bright smile on his face and an even brighter poem in his mind.

This is probably why Jimmy Carter, the 39th president of the United States, said, "The most extraordinary person I have ever known in my life was Mattie Stepanek." It is also why Mattie was asked to share his heartsong on shows including *The Oprah Winfrey Show*, *Good Morning America*, and *Larry King Live*. (Mattie said that if he could have made up the perfect show, it would include either the Simpsons or Weird Al Yankovic saying funny things about him.)

USA
population: 298 million
capital: Washington, D.C.

Mattie Stepanek liked Mike Meyers and Jim Carey. His favorite colors were sunset and elf green. He rooted for the Baltimore Orioles and the Washington Redskins. He passed away June 22, 2004. He was 14 years old.

Mattie said he wrote his heartsongs in order to "help others understand peace, so we can one day have it. We have to make peace an attitude. Then we have to make it a habit. Finally, we must decide to live peace, to share it around the world — not just talk about it. We each have an equal purpose, whether that purpose is big or small."

This was his heartsong.

What is yours?

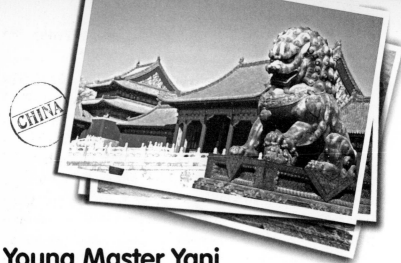

Young Master Yani
WANG YANI

When Wang Yani was three years old, she snuck into her father's painting studio. Animal-hair brushes were wrapped in cloth and jars of black liquid ink lined the walls. Sheets of handmade rice paper were stacked in piles and paintings hung from wires that crossed the ceiling. She smelled fresh ink drying on one of her father's paintings in the corner.

Yani wandered through the studio. She rubbed the brushes against her cheek and picked up jars of ink that could leave a black stain almost as powerful as a tattoo. If you have ever explored someplace new or dreamed of discovering a secret door into your own fantasyland, then you know how she felt. Finally, Yani found herself standing right in front of her father's finished painting, holding a paintbrush and a jar of ink.

What do you think she did?

Actually, she painted a huge black monkey right over the top of her father's finished work! Of course, this is right when her father walked in and Yani was caught black-handed. "Papa, I was helping you paint," she said. "I want to paint and paint!"

As you might guess, her father's first reaction was horror—Yani had destroyed his painting! But when her father showed the painting to his friends in their village of Gongcheng, China, they all agreed—the young girl's work was absolutely amazing! Rather than punishing her, Yani's father gave her a set of paints and brushes so she could make her own xieyi ("shay-e") paintings.

Xieyi painting uses big brush strokes of permanent ink. If you mess up, you have to throw the painting away and start all over again. Xieyi artists try to use only a few, perfect lines to put their feelings on paper. Most people believe you can't learn to be a great xieyi painter, but that you have to be born with a special talent for it. And Wang Yani certainly had talent.

One critic who saw her paintings said, "Yani's work is uninhibited genius. It's almost unbelievable that a youngster did these lovely, exciting works of art." An older Chinese painter gave up his brushes after seeing Yani's work because he felt his work could never equal the beauty of hers.

Wang Yani loved to visit the zoo. After visiting, this is what she did:

First, she sat cross-legged with her eyes closed in front of a piece of rice paper, which was

Yani has amazing skills!

stretched out on the floor in front of her. She tried to picture exactly what she wanted to paint and sat as long as it took to get the image just right in her mind. To her, this was the most important step. If she could imagine something first, she knew she would be able to draw it. Then she would open her eyes and in a quick motion she would grab a brush, dab it in ink, and get to work. One heavy stroke might become the trunk of a tree. Next, she might twist the brush to a fine tip and slide it gently across the paper to make a bird's long beak. She mixed colors to create deep reds and browns, which she dropped carefully onto the paper to make flower blossoms and slender branches. Her paintings were huge, so she stepped and crawled quietly around the paper, her eyebrows knit in concentration. When her painting

CHINA
population: 1.3 billion
capital: Beijing

was finished, she used a red stamp to put her name in the lower corner. It only took half an hour to finish. When she was done, Yani would sit down with her eyes closed in the same position as when she started.

It was as if she had been in a half-hour-long trance—as if somebody else had been painting and only when Yani opened her eyes would she really see her art for the first time. It's like waking up in the morning and finding you created a beautiful piece of art in your sleep. In this way, Yani painted flowers, cats, dragons, roosters, children, fish—and especially monkeys.

By the time she was four, Yani had her first painting exhibit in China. By the age of six, she had produced over 4,000 paintings. Since then, she has had art shows in Japan, England, Germany, and the United States. Wherever she has been, people have been amazed by the perfect technique and playful emotion in her art.

If you like to paint, here is some advice from a pro: "When you pick up a brush, don't even ask anyone for help, because the most wonderful thing about painting is being left alone with your imagination. I do not paint to get praise from others, but to play a game of endless joy."

You can read more about Wang Yani in the book *Wang Yani: Longing to Paint* by Anne Sibley O'Brien.

Snail Paint

VAISHALI KIRAN GROVER

One day when Vaishali Kiran Grover was 11, she was watering her family's papaya tree when she noticed something strange. "There were a lot of empty snail shells at the base of this tree," Vaishali recalled. "So I was wondering why there were so many empty shells under this tree and not underneath an avocado tree or a mango tree or anything like that."

Why did she care about empty snail shells under a tree, you might ask. Well, in addition to her love of flying kites on the beaches of Miami, Florida, with her dad, Vaishali also loved science. And that's what scientists do—they notice weird things and then wonder about them. And *why did shells under a papaya tree matter anyway,* you may wonder. Well, Vaishali didn't know why they mattered, or if they mattered at all. But like a true scientist, she decided that answering the question was the first step to finding out. Later, she would see if anything could be done with the information.

After doing some research, Vaishali learned that papayas contain something called *papain,* which some people use to tenderize meat. She thought that if this papain could make meat soft, maybe it could have something to do with the empty snail shells, too. To test her theory, she whipped up dried papaya bait and set it out for the snails. At the same time, she set out commercial snail bait made from pesticides. This is another thing scientists do—they experiment.

Turns out her experiment solved the mystery of the empty shells! Shortly after the snails ate the dried papaya, the papain in the fruit "immobilized" them—meaning the snails became snail juice. Not only did the papain kill the snails, but it did so faster and less expensively than the commercial pesticide. (Pesticides are often used to kill, well . . . pests.) And Vaishali's fruit-based snail bait was much more environmentally friendly than chemical-based pesticides.

Vaishali entered her work in an international science and engineering fair and was one of 40 students in the United States invited to Washington, D.C., to compete for the Young Scientist of the Year award. Vaishali was not named the young scientist of the year, but she did earn the Smithsonian Young Naturalist Award, which is given to the finalist whose work is the most important to the environment.

Many scientists would have been happy to stop right there. She had, after all, found a better way to keep snails out of gardens around the world. But Vaishali found herself thinking more and more about pesticides. What else used pesticides?

Living in Miami, Vaishali spent a lot of time near the ocean. She loved to stand on the beach and watch huge ships coming and going, and the scientist in her wanted to know as much as she could about the ships. So she did some research and learned, for instance, that ship bottoms were coated with *antifouling paint* to keep barnacles and other sea life from growing on them. Basically, antifouling paint is made up of something to kill barnacles and something sticky and waterproof to attach it to the hull of the boat. The stuff used to kill barnacles has always been made of chemicals and metals that are pretty nasty.

The big problem is that antifouling paint rubs off. Over time, as the paint rubs off, all the nasty stuff ends up in the water and makes its way into the silt at the bottom of the ocean. As you can imagine, the creatures that live in the silt at the bottom of the ocean don't like sharing their space with cancer-causing chemicals and metals. Today the U.S. Navy uses an antifouling paint that has to be replaced every 12 to 18 months. That means in a little over a year, enough paint to coat the bottom of every ship in the Navy leaks into the environment.

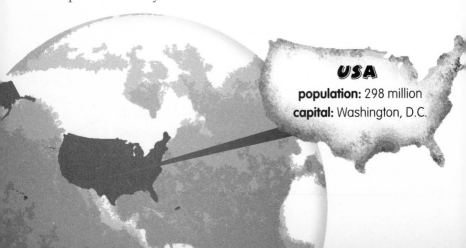

USA
population: 298 million
capital: Washington, D.C.

Vaishali figured that a barnacle was pretty much just an underwater snail, and she wondered whether papain would have the same effect on barnacles as it had on the snails she found at the base of her papaya tree.

Hmmmm. . . . Vaishali had gone from noticing a problem to wondering about it. She had thought of a possible solution, and now it was time for another experiment! On the beach, she found an old piece of metal with barnacles growing all over it. Vaishali put this chunk of metal in a bucket of saltwater and added a bunch of papaya. The result: The barnacles died! When Vaishali combined papaya with sticky tar, she had an antifouling paint that wouldn't mess up the environment.

In 2003, Vaishali Kiran Grover's Ship Shape Enzyme-Based Antifouling Paint won the Intel Foundation Achievement Award as well as awards from the U.S. Environmental Protection Agency, United Technologies Corporation, the U.S. Navy, and the U.S. Coast Guard. After that, the U.S. Navy said they would stop using toxic antifouling paint by the year 2008 and use a papain-based one instead.

Today, Vaishali Kiran Grover is at Northwestern University in Chicago, where she studies science and plants in hopes of becoming a seed engineer. No matter what she decides to do when she finishes school, you can be sure she will be wondering about the world and using her skills as a scientist to help solve its problems.

How will you use your skills?

Total barnacle juice!

A NOTE FROM THE AUTHOR

I hope you have enjoyed this book of young heroes from around the world. I first got the idea for *The Doggy Dung Disaster & Other True Stories* after visiting my wife's sixth-grade class. Like students in many social studies classes, the kids were studying heroes. But while the students had all picked admirable people to research, few had been able to find heroes they really connected with. Everybody was much older, most of the information about them was totally boring, and the things those heroes did seemed impossible.

In speaking and emailing with Kruti, both Ryans, Farliz, Henry, Amy, Vaishali, Mawi, and others, I was amazed by their accomplishments and surprised to find they are just regular people. My hope in writing this book was, first, that you would have fun reading these stories and, second, that somewhere along the way you would say, *Wow, that person sounds just like me!* In fact, the young people in this book *are* just like you. They happened to do these heroic things, but it could just as easily be your name on these pages.

I also wanted this book to help people see that heroism is universal. I lived in Bergen (Norway) and in Fontainebleau (France) when I was growing up, and have since traveled to many places in the world. No matter where we live or what language we speak, we are all working for the same things and we face many of the same challenges. Some of these challenges require regular people to become heroes.

Finally, if you have stories of young people doing heroic things—either about you or about people you know—I would love to hear them! You can write to me at the address below:

GARTH SUNDEM
c/o Free Spirit Publishing
217 Fifth Avenue North, Suite 200
Minneapolis, MN 55401-1299

Or you can email me:
help4kids@freespirit.com

BIBLIOGRAPHY

The Doggy Dung Disaster: Haruka Maruno

"Haruka Maruno: Hero for the Planet." *Time* 2000 Earth Day special edition. April–May 2000.

Web Japan. "Japanese Girl Named 'Hero for the Planet.'" www.web-japan.org/kidsweb/news/00-06/haruka.html (accessed October 18, 2005).

The Longest Walk: Omar Castillo Gallegos

United Nations Environment Programme. *The Global 500 Roll of Honour for Environmental Achievement:* p. 91. 2003.

Wikipedia.com. "*Rainforest.*" www.en.wikipedia.org/wiki/Rainforest (accessed March 19, 2006).

Zak, Monica. *Save My Rainforest*. Second edition. Volcano Press. 1989.

Turtle Power: Henry Cilley

Brown, Alison C. "Young Activist Aids Marsh and Blanding's Turtles." *Chicago Wilderness.* Summer 2003.

Cilley, Katherine. Telephone interview. September 13, 2005.

"Congrats Again to Henry, Defender of Turtles." *McHenry County Schools Environmental Education News.* March 2003.

Plastic Bags Sacked: Harshit Agrawal

Action for Nature. "2005 International Young Eco-Hero Awards." www.actionfornature.org/eco-hero (accessed November 5, 2005).

Global Village News and Resources. "International Young Eco Hero Awards." September 2005. www.gvnr.com/102/2. htm (accessed November 5, 2005).

Karthik, M. "Young Green Crusaders in B'Lore." *The New Observer*. December 16, 2002.

Roach, John, and Sara Ives. "Are Plastic Grocery Bags Sacking the Environment?" *National Geographic News*. September 2, 2003. www.news.nationalgeographic.com/ news/2003/09/0902_030902_plasticbags.html (accessed November 5, 2006).

Thakur, Panchalee. "Little Eco Friends Make a Big Difference." *The Times of India*. City Supplement: *Bangalore Times*. July 24, 2003.

Turtle Trax. "The Leatherback Turtle." www.turtles.org/ leatherd.htm (accessed November 5, 2005).

Show Me the Water! Amy Beal

Beal, Amy. Email interview. May 17, 2006.

Future Leaders. "The Island of San Salvatore: A Letter by Amy Beal." www.futureleaders.com.au/index. php?page=award_letter.htm (accessed May 18, 2006).

Governor's Leadership Foundation Alumni. www.savethemurray.com (accessed May 18, 2006).

Nationals, The. "Congratulations to Young Australian of the Year Finalists." November 27, 2003. www.nationals.org. au/news/default.asp?action-article&ID=161 (accessed May 18, 2006).

Nexus: Future Faces. Australian Broadcasting Corporation. April 14, 2006. abcasiapacific.com/nexus/futurefaces/s1583995.htm (accessed May 18, 2006)

"Success for Flinders Young Achievers." www.flinders.edu.au/news/articles/?oc06v13s11 (accessed May 18, 2006).

Comic Book Hero: Aika Tsubota

"Aika's Secrets of the Earth." ESCAP Virtual Conference. October 29, 2003. United Nations Economic and Social Commission for Asia and the Pacific. www.unescap.org/drpad/vc/conference/ex_jp_1_ase.htm (accessed October 19, 2005).

Collard III, Sneed B. *Acting for Nature: What Young People Around the World Have Done to Protect the Environment.* First edition. Berkeley: Heyday Books, 2000.

"Musical Inspired by Girl's Pro-Earth Comic ON Show at Expo." *Kyodo News.* May 19, 2005.

United Nations Environment Programme. *The Global 500 Roll of Honour for Environmental Achievement:* p. 81. 2003.

Top of the World: Santosh Yadav

Jayakrishnan, E. "Santosh Yadav: India's Everest Heroine." *Sify News.* May 26, 2003. www.sify.com/news/fullstory.php?id=13157470&vsv=722 (accessed October 18, 2005).

Mukherjee, Sanjeeb. "The Toughest Test of Endurance." *The Tribune.* June 9, 2002. www.tribuneindia.com/2002/20020609/spectrum/main4.htm (accessed October 18, 2005).

Salam, Ziya U. "On Top of the World at Baluchi!" *The Hindu.* May 29, 2003. www.hinduonnet.com/thehindu/ p/2003/05/29/stories/20033052901110400.htm (accessed October 18, 2006).

When Small Voices Unite: Farliz Calle and the Colombian Children's Peace Movement

Terzani, Anna. "Peace Child: Farliz Calle. Justice Education Forum 2004–2005. www.gallerie.net/issue5/persona/ peacechild.htm (accessed November 4, 2005).

Jewell, Wendy. "Peacemaker Hero: Peace Children." www.myhero.com/myhero/asp?hero=colombiaChildren (accessed November 4, 2005).

"Seeds of Peace: Young People in Colombia." The State of the World's Children 2000. www.unicef.org/sowc00/ panel5.htm (accessed November 4, 2005).

Sellers, Jeff M. "A Child Shall Lead Them." *Christianity Today.* December 3, 2001.

Come Together: Ivan Sekulovic and Petrit Selimi

"Global Youth Peace and Tolerance Awards 1999." www. y2kyouth.org/Global/award02.html (accessed November 4, 2005).

My Hero. "Peacemakers." www.myhero.com/myhero/ hero.asp?hero=postpessimists (accessed November 4, 2005).

Selimi, Petrit. "Letter From Pristina." Center for Democracy and Reconcilliation in Southeast Europe Bulletin Board. April 9, 2000. www.nettime.org/Lists-Archives/nettime-1- 0004/msg00059.html (accessed November 4, 2005).

Thorup Ph.D., Cathryn L. "What Works in Tolerance Among Balkan Children and Youth." International Youth Foundation 2003.

United Nations Interim Administration Mission in Kosovo. "Fire Fighters Control Blaze at Pristina Sports Complex." February 26, 2000. www.unmikonline.org/press/press/pr171.html (accessed November 4, 2005).

Get Up, Stand Up: Malika Sanders
Jewell, Wendy. "Community Hero: Malika Sanders." My Hero. www.myhero.com/myhero/hero.asp?hero=M_sanders (accessed November 4, 2005).

Sanders, Malika. "Get Your Vote On." YES! Spring 2002.

Themba, Makani. "Notorious Racist Mayor Challenged: Selma's Unfinished March to Freedom." *ColorLines: Race Culture Action.* August 25, 2000.

Forefront. "USA: Malika Asha Sanders." www.forefrontleaders.org/partners/north-america/malika-asha-sanders (accessed November 4, 2005).

Living Proof: Jean-Dominic Leversque-Rene
"Environmental Directive ED 4003-4/02: Directive to Eliminate the Use of Pesticides for Cosmetic Lawn Care Purposes on DND Properties." Canadian Services Personnel Support Agency. 2002.

Daborn, Lia. "Restricting Cosmetic Pesticide Use — An Idea Whose Time Has Come." *Eco Alert:* Volume 32, No. 2. June 2001.

Environmental Health Association of Nova Scotia. "A Young Crusader Speaks about Pesticides, Children, and Cancer." September 25, 2001. www.chebucto.ns.ca/Health/Nsaeha/sep01speak.html.

Environment News Service. "World Environment Day 2001: No Pesticides and Fresh Water for All." June 4, 2001. www.ens-newswire.com/ens/jun2001/2001-06-04-04.asp l (accessed October 19, 2005).

Lalonde, Michelle. "Montreal Takes Step Towards Banning All Pesticides." *The Montreal Gazette.* February 21, 2003.

Levesque-Rene, Jean-Dominic. "Finally Pesticide-Free on l'Ile Bizard." Canadians Against Pesticides. February 7, 2001. www.caps.20m.com/bizard.htm (accessed on October 19, 2005).

Wikipedia.com. "Royal Montreal Golf Club." www.en.wikipedia.org/wiki/Royal_Montreal_Golf_Club (accessed October 19, 2005).

Star Online, The. "The Pesticide Pest." June 5, 2001. www.kustem.edu.my/seatrue/news/star050601/index.html (accessed October 19, 2005).

Tvedten, Stephen. "Quebec Teen Honoured by UN Agency." Safe2Use. June 16, 2001. www.safe2use.com/ca-ipm/01-06-16.htm (accessed October 19, 2005).

United Nations Environment Programme. *The Global 500 Roll of Honor for Environmental Achievement:* p. 140. 2003.

From Rug Maker to Rescuer: Iqbal Masih

Wikipedia.com. "Iqbal Masih." www.en.wikipedia.org/
wiki/Iqbal_Masih (accessed October 18, 2005).

World's Children's Prize for the Rights of the Child, The.
"The World's Children's Prize for the Rights of the Child
2000: Iqbal Masih." www.childrensworld.org/page.
html?pid=53 (accessed October 18, 2005).

Hear That? Ryan Patterson

Anectdotage.com. "Ryan Patterson: Boy Genius."
www.anecdotage.com/index.php?aid=17733 (accessed
November 5, 2005).

"Best Inventions 2002: Braille Glove." *Time*. November 18,
2002.

Dean, Katie. "A Glove That Speaks Volumes."
Wired. January 28, 2002. www.wired.com/news/
gizmos/0,1452,4971600.html (accessed November 5, 2005).

National Institute on Deafness and Other Communication
Disorders. "Teenage Inventor Brings Sign-Translating Glove
to NIDCD." March 19, 2002. www.nidcd.nih.gov/news/
releases/02/3_19_02.htm (accessed November 5, 2005).

National Museum of Education. "The National Gallery for
America's Young Inventors: The 2002 Inductees." www.
nmoe.org/gallery/i02.htm (accessed November 5, 2005).

Pop Art: Junichi Ono

Marshall, Andrew. "Prodigies: So Bright (Asia: Small
Wonders)." *Time*. February 17, 2003.

Poskanzer, Barbara. "Spellbound by Tradition: Japan's Crown Prince and Prime Minister Lead Cheers at Opening Ceremonies." *Spirit.* Quarter 2, 2005.

Early Warning System: Tilly Smith
BBC.CO.UK. "Award for Tsunami Warning Pupil." September 9, 2005. News.bbc.co.uk/2/hi/uk_news/4229392.stm.

FoxNews.com. "Schoolgirl Saves Nearly 100 Lives." January 2, 2005. www.foxnews.com/story/0,2933,143093,00.html (accessed November 4, 2005).

Owen, James. "Tsunami Family Saved by Schoolgirl's Geography Lesson." *National Geographic News.* January 18, 2005.

Telegraph.co.uk. "Girl, 10, Used Geography Lesson to Save Lives." January 1, 2005. www.telegraph.co.uk/news/main.jhtml?xml=/news/2005/01/01/ugeog.xml&sSheet=/portal/2005/01/01/ixportaltop.html (accessed November 4, 2005)

Workers Unite! Chen Chiu-Mian
New York State Department of Health. www.health.state.ny.us (accessed November 4, 2005).

Taiwan Association for Victims of Occupational Injuries. www.tavoi.myweb.hinet.net (accessed November 4, 2005).

Taiwan Labor Front. www.labor.ngo.org.tw (accessed November 4, 2005).

Yiu, Cody. "Young activist finds politics to her liking." *Taipei Times.* July 5, 2004.

Sow What You Reap: P.B.K.L. Agyirey-Kwakye

Ennin, Emelia. "Adopting sustainable means of energy — A national challenge." Ghana Web. May 13, 2005. www.ghanaweb.com/GhanaHomePage/features/artikel.php?ID=81363 (accessed November 4, 2005).

Tenywa, Gerald. "Eucalyptus Tree Can Stave Off Timber and Fuel Wood Crisis." All Africa. August 23, 2005. www.allafrica.com/stories/200508230063.html (accessed November 4, 2005).

United Nations Environment Programme. *The Global 500 Roll of Honour for Environmental Achievement:* p. 120. 2003.

TakingITGlobal. "Youth Club for Nature Conservation." profiles.takingitglobal.org/ycnc (accessed November 4, 2005).

Ryan's Wells: Ryan Hreljac

Cook, Kathy. "Ryan's Well." *Reader's Digest Canada.* January 2001. www.readersdigest.ca/mag2001/01/ryan.html (accessed November 4, 2005).

Jewell, Wendy. "Lifesaver Hero: Ryan Hreljac." My Hero. www.myhero.com/myhero/hero.asp?hero=RYAN_HRELJAC (accessed November 4, 2005).

Back on the Board: Bethany Hamilton

BethanyHamilton.com. "Bio." www.bethanyhamilto.com/bio.html (accessed November 5, 2005).

CNN.com. "Then & Now: Bethany Hamilton." June 22, 2005. www.cnn.com/2005/US/05/09/cnn25.tan.hamilton (accessed November 5, 2005).

My Hero. "Child Hero: Bethany Hamilton." www.myhero. com/myhero/hero.asp?hero=Bethany_SJH_ (accessed November 5, 2005).

Skilling, Johanna. "Most Inspiring Person of the Year Award: Finalist: Bethany Hamilton." BeliefNet. www. beliefnet.com/story/137/story_13707_1.html (accessed November 5, 2005).

TenBruggencate, Jan. "Bethany Only Looking Ahead." *Honolulu Advertiser.* November 21, 2003.

Witness. "Partner Network—Africa: Abraham Gebreyesus, Eritrea." www.witness.org/index.php?option=com_content &task=blogcategory&id=55&Itemid=165&limit=5&limitstart =5 (accessed November 5, 2005).

A Wish to Breathe Free: Izidor Ruckel

Hannigan, Edward. "Former Romanian Orphan Vows to Return to Free Others." *Valley News.* November 19, 2004. www.temeculavalleynews.com/story.asp?story_ID=10774 (accessed November 5, 2005).

Kwak, Han. "Romanian Orphan's Road to Forgiveness." *The Press-Enterprise.* November 4, 2003.

Ruckel, Izidor, and Joan Bramsch, ed. *Abandoned for Life: The Incredible Story of One Romanian Orphan Hidden from the World* (eBook). ISBN 0-934334. 2002. Ruckel, Izidor. "My Story." www.izidor.org (accessed November 5, 2005).

The Matchless Girl of Matches: Fatema Begum

Kumar Barua, Susanta. "Poor and Destitute Working Children in Bangladesh." Submission by SRG Welfare

Society of Bangladesh to the CRC General Discussion Day on Implementing Child Rights in Early Childhood.

People's Health Movement. "Slum Dwellers—Fatema Begum." www.phmovement.org/voices/begum.html (accessed November 5, 2005).

Shahab, Sabrina. "I Am Fatema: A Story of a Girl from Bangladesh." Your True Hero. www.yourtruehero.org/content/hero/view_hero.asp?13469 (accessed November 5, 2005).

Underprivileged Children's Educational Program. "Fatema Begum: A Good Example of Struggle and Success." www.ucepbd.org/stories2.html (accessed November 5, 2005).

Lemons to Lemonade: Alexandra Scott
Alex's Lemonade Stand. www.alexslemonade.com (accessed November 5, 2005).

Barry, Ellen. "Love Triumphs: 6-Year-Old Becomes Hero to Band of Toddlers, Rescuers." *Houston Chronicle.* September 6, 2005.

Budoff, Carrie. "Girl's Lemonade Helps Cancer Fund." *Hartford Courant.* July 2, 2000.

"Courageous Child Unites Country." *Cincinnati Post.* June 11, 2004.

Klein, Michael. "Philadelphia Publisher Is Doing Its Bit for Alex's Lemonade Stand." *Philadelphia Inquirer.* May 19, 2005.

Schogol, Marc. "Lemonade Cause Known Far and Wide." *Philadelphia Inquirer*. August 4, 2003.

Schogol, Marc. "Selling Lemonade for Cancer Research." *Philadelphia Inquirer*. August 2, 2004.

New Land, a New Life: Mawi Asgedom
Asgedom, Mawi. *Of Beetles and Angels: A Boy's Remarkable Journey from Refugee Camp to Harvard*. Megan Tingley, 2002.

Bystander. "A Conversation with Mawi Asgedom" by Bella Stander. 2001. www.bellastander.com/writer/mawi.html (accessed November 5, 2005).

Goodnow, Cecelia. "A Moment with Mawi Asgedom, speaker/author." *Seattle Post Intelligencer*. September 16, 2003.

Hachette Book Group USA. "Author Interview: Mawi Asgedom." www.hachettebookgroupusa.com/authors/85/2560/interview15620.html (accessed November 5, 2005).

A Leg Up on the Competition: Rudy Garcia-Tolson
CANOE. "Garcia Leads Record Spree." September 19, 2004. www.slam.canoe.ca/Slam/Athletics/Games/2004/Parlympics/2004/09/20/636858.html (accessed November 5, 2005).

Garza, Xazmin. "Superkid Rudy Garcia Tolson lives every moment to the fullest." Salt Lake 2002 Paralympics. www.saltlake2002.paralympic.org/front_features/ceremonies/opening/tolson/one.html (accessed November 5, 2005).

Kostich, Alex. "Amputee Rudy Garcia-Tolson Takes Being a 12-Year-Old as Seriously as He Races." Active.com. July 16, 2001. www.active.com/story.cfm?story_id=7543&category= triathlon (accessed November 5, 2005).

Murphy, Austin. "Murphy's Law: And a Child Shall Lead Them." SI.com. November 18, 2002. www.sportsillustrated. cnn.com/features/siadventure/21/murphys_law (accessed November 5, 2005).

Ossur: Life Without Limitations. "Rudy Garcia-Tolson." December 2004. www.ossur.com/template110.asp/ pageID=1313 (accessed November 5, 2005).

See It to Believe It: Kruti Parekh
Parekh, Kruti. Email interview. September 21, 2005.

Parekh, Kruti. "Kruti Parekh." www.magickingdom4u.com (accessed November 5, 2005).

United Nations Environment Programme. *The Global 500 Roll of Honor for Environmental Achievement:* p. 127. 2003.

Outta This World: Christopher Paolini
Teenreads.com. "Author Profile: Christopher Paolini." September 2003. www.teenreads.com/authors/au-paolini-christopher.asp (accessed November 5, 2005).

Weich, Dave. "Philip Pullman, Tamora Pierce, and Christopher Paolini Talk Fantasy Fiction." Powells.com. www.powells.com/authors/paolini.html (accessed November 5, 2005).

Sports Hero: Nguyen Ngoc Truong Son

Marshall, Andrew. "Prodigies: So Bright! Small Wonders." *Time*. February 10, 2003. www.time.com/time/asia/covers/501030217.html (accessed November 5, 2005).

Onestopenglish.com. "Genius Reading A: Nguyen Ngoc Truong Son." www.onestopenglish.com/skills/Reading/reading_worksheets/genius_readings.pdf (accessed November 5, 2005).

Radio the Voice of Vietnam: Personalities. "International Chess Youth Prodigy Touches Gold for Vietnam." www.vov.org.vn (accessed November 5, 2005).

Uglychart.com. "Nguyen Ngoc Truong Son." February 7, 2005. www.uglychart.com/archives/2005/02/nguyen_ngoc_tru.html (accessed November 5, 2005).

"Vietnamese Boy May Enter Top 100 Chess Grandmasters." *Thanh Nien Daily*. December 27, 2004.

Beyond His Years: Mattie Stepanek

Hawkins, Jim. "Poet Hero: Mattie Stepanek."My Hero. www.myhero.com/myhero/hero.asp?hero=mattiestepanek (accessed on November 5, 2005).

MattieOnline.com. "Welcome to Mattie's Website!" www.mattieonline.com (accessed on November 5, 2005).

Muscular Dystrophy Association. "MDA's Mattie Is Nation's Best-Selling Author." January 25, 2002. www.mdausa.org/news/20125mattieNYT.html (accessed on November 5, 2005).

"Oprah Talks to Mattie." *Oprah Magazine*. November 2002.

Stepanek, Mattie. "My Name Is Mattie." My Hero. www.
myhero.com/myhero/hero.asp?hero=mattiestepanek
(accessed on November 5, 2005).

Young Master Yani: Wang Yani
"Brush Strokes of Genius." *Philadelphia Intelligencer.* June 7,
1989.

Gibbs, Kate. "Arthur M. Sackler Gallery: Smithsonian
Institution." *Washington Post.* November 29, 1989.

Goodrich, Warren. "A Hundred Monkeys and More."
Wellsboro Gazette. September 27, 1989.

Ho, Wai-Ching. *Yani: The Brush of Innocence.* Hudson Hills
Press.1989.

Miclat, Maningning. "The Visual Poetry of Chinese
Bamboo: Some Notes on Traditional Chinese Xieyi
Painting." University of the Phillipines Dillman. www.
ovcrd.upd.edu.ph (accessed on November 5, 2005).

My Hero. "Artist Hero: Wang Yani." www.myhero.com/
myhero/hero.asp?hero=w_yani (accessed on November 5,
2005).

O'Crowley, Peggy. "The Young Empress of Art." *The Bergen
County Record:* Lifestyle section. October 4, 1991.

Snail Paint: Vaishali Kiran Grover
American Association for the Advancement of Sciences.
"Slide Show — AAAS at EuroScience Open Forum, 2004:
Shirley Malcolm's Speech." www.aaas.org/news/releases/
2004/0831euro6malcolm.shtml (accessed November 5,
2005).

Australian Government Department of Defence: Defence Science and Technology Organisation. Department of Defence. "Anti-fouling paint a winner for marine environment." July 20, 2005. www.dsto.defence.gov.au (accessed on November 5, 2005).

Corrosion Doctors. "Antifouling Coatings." www.corrosion-doctors.org (accessed on November 5, 2005).

Grover, P.K. Telephone interview. September 28, 2005.

National Museum of Education. "The National Gallery for America's Young Inventors: Meet the 2004 Inductees." www.nmoe.org/gallery/i04htm (accessed on November 5, 2005).

Non-Resident Indians Online. "USA: NRI teens bag top US science awards." October 31, 2000. www.nriol.com (accessed on November 5, 2005).

Technology Administration. "Student Technology Roundtable: 2000 Event Program." www.technology.gov/Medal/p_educoutr.utm (accessed on November 5, 2005).

Population Information

Central Intelligence Agency. "The World Factbook 2006." www.cia.gov/cia/publications/factbook (accessed October 1, 2006).